Ralph Burkhardt

HOTCH POTCH

Lexicon of (un)useful
creative knowledge

1 *a collection containing a variety of sorts of things.*

2 *a thick soup or stew of vegetables or meat.*

These two definitions are from the Oxford Dictionary when you look up the word Hotchpotch and I am still not sure which one I prefer most. After collecting all those facts and anecdotes this book feels like a medley of favourite songs/facts, that you want to recommend/tell your friends. Just skip through, jump from one topic to another, get inspired by the connections that occur on a spread and dig deeper when something caught your attention. The selection is arbitrary and intended at the same time. Sometimes it's just a certain word that sounds remarkable and worth to remember.

Hotchpotch is organised like a dictionary, but with creative knowledge. Therefore the collection of facts in this book is limited and not anywhere close to an extensive compendium. Hotchpotch doesn't demand integrity which isn't possible anyway. Knowledge, whether it is useful or unuseful, keeps evolving and new facts and anecdotes pop up any second. Hotchpotch is more of a frozen extract of "creative facts" and I apologize for anyone or anything not included.

All informations in Hotchpotch are checked to the best of my belief, so let me know if something is missing or an incorrect year has made its way into the book. The input of you, the reader is more than welcome and you are allowed to contact me anytime.

After all, I would especially like to thank BIS Publishers and all people who made this book possible and granted me the rights to use a certain picture. A special thanks goes to Lance Wyman, April Greiman and particularly George Lois who was so kind to write his own entry.

And now have fun browsing through Hotchpotch!

Ralph Burkhardt
Germany, 2017

A

Steve Averill

A Most dictionaries list the alphabet letter "A" as the first word.

Aalto Vase, the is a piece of glassware created by Alvar Aalto and his wife Aino Marsio that has become an iconic piece of Finnish design. The Aalto vase became also known as the Savoy Vase because it was one of a range of custom furnishings created for the luxury Savoy restaurant in Helsinki. Less known is that the vase was actually called "Eskimåkvinnans skinnbyxa" (the Eskimo woman's leather breech) and that the design was inspired by the shape of finish fjords.

Aardvark Discounting "A" as a real word, the first word in a dictionary is Aardvark, a medium-sized, burrowing, nocturnal mammal native to Africa.

Ball Chair, 1963. Design: Eerio Aarnio.
© www.ambientedirect.com.

Aarnio, Eerio is a Finnish interior designer, who is best known for his innovative designs, like his Ball Chair (1963). His designs are considered Modernist or Space Age

and could often be seen as part of sets in science-fiction films.

Abrogans is a Middle Latin/Old High German glossary from the 8th century. It is regarded as the oldest preserved book in the German language. The glossary contains round about 3,670 Old High German words in over 14,600 examples.

Accolade Also known as curly parenthesis or nose clip. Accolades can mainly be found in German-speaking countries.

Accordion fold Binding term for two or more parallel folds that will open up like an accordion. Maps and leaflets often use accordion folds.

Acrobat A product developed by Adobe systems to create a PDF (Portable Document Format) file. Acrobat, available for Microsoft Windows and Apple only, can create, view, export, publish and print documents.

Acronym A word formed from the initial letters of the words in a name or phrase, for example FAQ (Frequently Asked Questions) or GIF (Graphics Interchange Format).

Acrostic A series of lines in which certain letters, usually the first in each line, form a name or message when read in sequence. In Lewis Carroll's final chapter of "Through the Looking-Glass", you can find an acrostic of the real Alice's name: Alice Pleasance Liddell.

Action office, the is a series of furniture, first introduced in 1964 and designed by Robert Propst for Herman Miller. The Action Office system was designed to promote productivity, privacy, and health in

The Aalto Vase, 1937. Design: Alvar Aalto. © Iittala.

an efficient use of space. The Action office series evolved into the today well-known cubicle system, a concept of flexible, semi-enclosed workspaces.

Adbusters The Adbusters Media Foundation is a global network of artists, activists, writers, pranksters, students, educators and entrepreneurs. Their aim is to fight back against the takeover of our psychological, physical and cultural environments by commercial forces. The anti-consumerist and pro-environment organization was founded in Vancouver, British Columbia in 1989 by Kalle Lasn and Bill Schmalz.

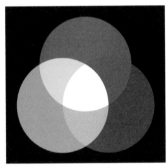

Additive primary colours.

Additive colour is colour created by mixing a number of different light colours. Adding red to green yields yellow; adding all three primary colours (Red, Green and Blue) together yields white.

Adenauer, Konrad The former German Chancellor has also been known as Inventor and Designer. He designed a darning Egg with interior lighting. The mushroom-shaped object was manufactured

by AEG, a major German electrical appliances manufacturer.

Adidas The stripes positioned at 60° to the sole of the famous shoe company originally were meant to stabilize the middle-foot section. They became a very strong visual instead.

Adidas logo. © Adidas.

Adobe The name of the company comes from Adobe Creek in Los Altos, California, which ran behind the houses of both of the company's founders, John Warnock and Chuck Geschke.

Adorno, Theodor W. The philosopher effectively mused on the lettering on the spines of books: "Long-running distaste of books whose titles have been printed lengthwise on the spines. Should be crosswise on humane ones."

Adshel An Adshel is a poster that is integrated into the structure of a bus shelter. In other countries this type of product is also called Abribus or City-Light-Poster (CLP).

Advertorial An advertorial is an advertisement that is designed to look like editorial, usually with short headlines, small photos and text set in columns.

AEG In 1907, Peter Behrens designed the entire corporate identity (logotype, product design, packaging design and so on) for AEG Turbine Factory. This was actually the first overall corporate identity ever made for a company.

AEG company logo, 1908. Design: Peter Behrens.

Aeron chair, 1994. Design: Don Chadwick and Bill Stumpf.

Aeron chair, the has been called "America's best-selling chair" (as of 2010). The Aeron chair is an office chair designed by Don Chadwick and Bill Stumpf in 1994. As described by Galen Kranz: "one of the secrets of the success of that chair was finding that fabric they called 'pellicle'."

Agha, Mehemed Fehmy was a Russian-born Turkish graphic designer who worked for magazines like Vogue and Vanity Fair. In 1930,

he was the first known art director who introduced the double page spread, bleed photos and sans-serif typefaces, like Futura, in Editorial design.

Aicher, Otl was a German graphic designer and typographer who is best known for having designed the pictograms for the 1972 Summer Olympics in Munich. Unfortunately Aicher died while cutting the lawn of his property in Rotis in Southern Germany on September 1st 1991. He was hit by a motorcycle while he reversed into a street with his rideable lawnmower.

Affair of the Placards, the was an incident in 1534 in Paris and other cities, in which French Protestants put up placards, or posters, attacking the Catholic mass.

Affiche The French expression affiche means display, poster, bill or placard. There is also a special paper for outdoor posters called "Affichenpapier".

AIGA stands for American Institute of Graphic Arts, a professional organization for design, founded in 1914.

Agate is a term used originally to designate 5.5 point size type. It is considered to be the smallest point size that can be printed on newsprint and remain legible, depending on the typeface though.

Albers, Anni (1899–1994) was an American textile artist and printmaker. She is probably the best known textile artist of the 20th century. Besides her textile work she created striking jewellery inspired by the treasures of ancient Mexico and made from household objects, such as hairpins, washers and a sink strainer.

Albers, Josef was a photographer, designer, typographer, printmaker, poet and husband of Anni Albers but he is best remembered for his work as an abstract painter and theorist. Most famous of all are the hundreds of paintings and prints that make up the series "Homage to the Square". In this series, Albers explored chromatic interactions with nested squares. He only used industrially produced colours. That's why he often recorded the product number of each colour on the back of his works.

Albus, Volker is an architect and designer who wove a carpet out of ads for cheap carpets. The "Real Nepal Carpet" came out in 1993 in an edition of ten. The handtufted pure-wool carpet has been showcased in numerous exhibitions.

The "Real Nepal Carpet", 1993. Design: Albus Volker. © Quittenbaum Kunstauktionen.

Aldine Press was the name of the printing office started by Aldus Manutius in 1494 in Venice, from which were issued the celebrated Aldine editions of the classics (Latin and Greek masterpieces plus a few more modern works). The first book that was dated and printed under his name appeared in 1495. The press was the first to issue printed books in the small octavo size, similar to that of a modern paperback, intended for portability and ease of reading. Their logo of the anchor and dolphin is represented today in symbols and names used by some modern publishers such as Doubleday. The anchor was a symbol of reliability and solidity, the dolphin a symbol for swiftness.

Aldus leaf The Aldus leaf is an ornament form, which is named after the Italian publisher Aldus Manutius. He used the heart-shaped leaf as decoration in his books. Another name for the Aldus Leaf is Hedera after the Latin name for ivy, which had a certain similarity because of its leaf shape. However, the Aldus Leaf was increasingly stylized over time to the shape of a heart. Typographically seen it belongs to the Fleurons, the flower-like decorative ornaments.

Aldine Press logo.

Aldus Manutius was an Italian humanist who became a printer and publisher. He founded the Aldine Press at Venice in 1494. He is also called "the Elder" to distinguish him from his grandson Aldus Manutius.

Aleph is the first letter of the Semitic abjads. It is actually derived from an Egyptian hieroglyph depicting an ox's head and gave rise to the Greek Alpha, and hence the Latin and Cyrillic A.

Phoenician aleph.

Alignment The adjustment of arrangement of a text or an image: left, right, centred, etc.

Alpha channel, the represents the degree of transparency (or opacity) of a colour (i.e., the red, green and blue channels). It is used to determine how a pixel is rendered when blended with another.

Alphanumeric Refers to any system that combines letters and numbers.

American Quarto Beyond North America, the Letter page size is in fact known as American Quarto.

Two different Ampersand symbols.

Ampersand An ampersand is a logogram ("&") representing the conjunction word "and". The amper-

sand can be traced back to the 1st century A.D. and the Old Roman cursive, in which the letters E and T ("et" is Latin for and) occasionally were written together to form a ligature.

Amplitude Extra Compressed Ultra

Amplitude Extra Compressed Ultra, 2003. Design: Christian Schwartz.

Amplitude is a typeface designed by Christian Schwartz in 2003 with many different weights and widths. When Schwartz started working on the Extra Compressed font, though, he had a very particular area of application in mind: "I'd like to see it used at the bottom of film posters, for the credits, which are always set very tightly and almost impossible to read."

Amplitude modulation describes a continuous tone imagery that contains an infinite range of colours or greys. The halftone process reduces visual reproductions to an image that is printed with only one colour of ink, in dots of differing size.

Analog Proof A proof, also known as (prepress Proof) that uses ink jet, toner powder, dyes, overlays, photographic, film, or other methods to give an idea of what the finished product should look like.

Anchor Point Anchor points allow the user to manipulate a path's shape or direction by clicking the point and moving it in a direction. They appear along the beginning of a path, at every curve, and at the end of a path.

Anglepoise lamp A balanced-arm lamp designed in 1932 by British

11

designer George Carwardine. The lamp has become an icon of British design and a prototype for workbench lamps to come. Anglepoise is French and means balanced angular.

Original 1227 Anglepoise desk lamp, 1932. Design: George Carwardine.
© www.ambientedirect.com.

Animated GIF A small animation based on continuous GIF images, giving the impression of movement or action. The Graphics Interchange Format was introduced by CompuServe in 1987.

Anna G The facial expression and the thin, long-limbed body Alessandro Mendini designed for the bottle opener is said to be inspired by the female artist and designer Anna Gili, Mendini and Alessi's good friend, that gave the name to the corkscrew.

ANSI Abbreviation for American National Standards Institution, the equivalent of the DIN (German Industry Standard).

Anti-aliasing may refer to any of a number of techniques to combat the problems of aliasing in a sampled signal such as a digital image.

Anti-Design was a design and art movement originating in Italy and lasting from the years 1966–1980. The Anti-Design movement was a reaction against the perfectionist aesthetics of Modernism. Where Modernism followed the idea of objects being permanent, Anti-Designers wanted objects to be temporary, and be replaced by something new and more functional. They wanted people to think about the objects they were buying. Some of the key designers were Ettore Sottsass Jr. and the Radical Design groups Archigram and Superstudio.

Antiqua Typefaces that are designed between about 1470 and 1600, specifically those by Nicolas Jenson and the Aldine roman commissioned by Aldus Manutius. Antiqua letterforms were modelled on a synthesis of Roman inscriptional capitals and Carolingian writing.

ABCDEFGHIJK LMNOPQRSTU VWXYZÀÅÉÎ ÕØÜ&123456 7890($£€.,!?)

Antique, 1815. Design: Vincent Figgins.

Antique was the name of the first Slab Serif typeface presented to the public in 1815. Antique was designed by Vincent Figgins, who also made many sans serif typefaces.

Antique Olive is a humanist sans-serif typeface designed in the early 1960s by French typographer Roger Excoffon. It was usually created while Excoffon was working on a

Anna G bottle opener, 1994. Design: Alessandro Mendini. © Alessi.

new logo and advertising poster for Air France. They called the result Antique Olive; Antique being the French term for sans-serif.

ABCDEFGHIJKL MNOPQRSTUV WXYZÅÅÆÎÔØÜ abcdefghijklm nopqrstuvwxy zàâéîôøü&1234 567890($£.,!?)

Antique Olive Nord, 1960s. Design: Roger Excoffon.

Aperture Opening at the end of an open counter of a letter.

And

Aperture.

Apex The point at the top of a character such as an uppercase A.
Appendix An additional information provided at the end of a book or article.
Apple Macintosh If you open up the case of the original Apple Macintosh, you will find 47 written signatures, which are from each member of the Apple's Macintosh division in 1982.
Arad, Ron is an Israeli industrial designer, artist, and architect. His iconic Big Easy Chair from 1989 was featured in Michael Jackson's video Scream.
Architecture Between 1912 and 1948 architecture was an Olympic

sport. The idea goes back to Pierre de Coubertin, the founder of the modern Olympic movement. Medals were awarded for work, that is related to sport in the five fields of architecture, literature, music, painting and sculpture. These so called art competitions were withdrawn from the program of the Olympic Games in 1954.

ARCHITYPE VAN DOESBURG

Architype Van Doesburg typeface, 1919.

Architype Van Doesburg is a geometric sans-serif typeface originally designed in 1919 by Theo van Doesburg, a cofounder of the De Stijl art movement. Each character is based upon a square divided into a raster of 25 smaller squares.

Volt

Arm.

Arm A horizontal stroke not connected on one or both ends.
Arntz, Gerd was a German Modernist artist (1900 – 1988) known for his popular black and white woodcuts. In 1929 Arntz started working at the "Gesellschafts- und Wirtschaftsmuseum" (Social and Economic Museum) directed by Neurath in Vienna, where he designed around 4000 signs. These signs symbolized key data from industry, demographics, politics, and economy. They were used for

the visual language Isotype (International System Of TYpographic Picture Education).

Arts & Crafts movement, the was one of the most influential design movements of modern times which started in Britain around 1880. It had a strong influence on the Arts in Europe until it was displaced by Modernism in the 1930s.

Arts & Architecture was an American magazine about design, architecture, landscape, and arts. It was published and edited by John Entenza and David Travers from 1929–1967 and had a huge impact on American modernism.

Art Director Individual person responsible for the selection, execution, production etc. of graphic art.

Fish

Ascender.

Ascender An upward stroke found on lowercase letters that extends above the typeface's x-height.

ASCII is a well-known character-encoding scheme. The American Standard Code for Information Interchange, short ASCII, represents all kinds of text in computers, communications equipment, and other devices that use text. Most character-encoding schemes are based on ASCII, though they support many additional characters. ASCII was the most common character encoding on the WWW until 2007, when it was surpassed by UTF-8, which includes ASCII as a subset.

Asterisk An asterisk (*) is a typographical symbol or glyph that resembles a conventional image of a star. It is used as censorship or to correct one's spelling, in which case it appears after or before the corrected word.

Asymmetrical This is when graphics and/or text are not identical on both sides of a central line.

At sign The @-sign, normally read aloud as "at", also commonly called the at symbol or commercial at, is originally an accounting and commercial invoice abbreviation meaning "at a rate of". Whatever the origin of the @-symbol is, the history of its usage is better known: it has long been used in Spanish and Portuguese as an abbreviation of arroba, a unit of weight equivalent to 25 pounds, and derived from the Arabic expression of "a quarter".

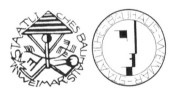

Left: First Bauhaus Seal, 1919. Design: Johannes Auerbach. Right: Oskar Schlemmer, 1922.

Auerbach, Johannes Ilmari was a Jewish painter and sculptor who was responsible for the first Bauhaus seal in 1919, chosen in a student design competition. Style and symbolism expressed the medieval and craft affinities of the early Bauhaus. The initial logo was replaced by an updated version, designed by Oskar Schlemmer in 1922.

ASCII picture of myself.

Authagraph is a unique world map projection, that is based on Buckminster Fuller's Dymaxion map. It was actually designed by Japanese architect Hajime Narukawa. The new innovative projection method can convert a full spherical image, such as a globe, on a rectangular display without any overlaps and gaps.

Avant Garde typeface, 1968. Design: Herb Lubalin.

Avant Garde is a font family based on the logo font used in the Avant Garde magazine. Herb Lubalin devised the logo concept and its companion headline typeface, then he and Tom Carnase, a partner in Lubalin's design firm, worked together to transform the idea into a full-fledged typeface.

Averill, Steve is an Irish graphic artist, designer, writer, and former punk rock vocalist who has designed all the album covers for the Irish band U2. Averill also brainstormed U2 as their band name.

B42 The Gutenberg Bible (aka the 42-line Bible, the Mazarin Bible or the B42) was the first major book printed using mass-produced movable type. It marked the start of the "Gutenberg Revolution" and the age of the printed book in the West. The last sale of a complete Gutenberg Bible took place in 1978. It fetched $2.2 million. The folio size, 307×445 mm, has the ratio of 1.45:1. The printed area had the same ratio, and was shifted out of the middle to leave a 2:1 white margin, both horizontally and vertically.

Gutenberg Bible of the New York Public Library. © NYC Wanderer (Kevin Eng).

Baas, Maarten is a Dutch designer who is best known for his rebellious and playful work. His graduation series called "Smoke", which consists of burned furniture, became a big success and even featured Angelina Jolie sitting in a "Smoke Armchair". The "Smoke" series is produced by international design company Moooi, based in The Netherlands.

Babel Fish was Yahoo's free web-based multilingual translation app. The internet service derived its name from the Babel fish, a fictional species in Douglas Adams's book and radio series "The Hitchhiker's Guide to the Galaxy". The name of the fictional creature refers to the biblical account of the confusion of languages that arose in the city of Babel.

Backslant

Helvetica backslanted.

Backslant An effect in typography in which the letters slant to the left instead of to the right as in italics.

Backslash The backslash (\) is a typographical mark used mainly in computing. It was introduced into ASCII by Bob Bemer in 1961.

Bad Break A break that causes awkward reading. Refers to widows or orphans in text copy.

Balla, Giacomo was an artist and poet who became part of the Futurist Manifesto. Before that he declared in 1913: "Balla is dead", sold all his paintings and started to design.

Ballpoint pen One refill is enough for a line of 5,000 – 10,000 meters.

ball

Ball terminal.

Ball terminal A circular shape at the end of a stroke on certain letterforms of some serif fonts.

Bang In the 50s, typesetting manuals and secretarial dictation in theUS referred to the exclamation mark as "bang". This term could derive from comic books where the

Smoke Dining Chair by Maarten Baas. © moooi.

"!" appeared in dialogue balloons to represent a gun being fired.

Qwerty Issue 1, "For those who get their fingers dirty", 1991. © Stephen Banham.

Banham, Stephen is an Australian typographer and type designer who published a series of six experimental spiral-bound issues, called Qwerty. There was very little happening in Australia in terms of typography in 1990 and with international interest in Qwerty, he could soon present his work to a wider audience.

Bantjes, Marian is a Canadian designer, who became famous for her detailed typographic and highly ornamental design style. Less familiar is that Bantjes lives on an isolated property on Bowen Island, in Howe Sound off Vancouver.

Bar The horizontal or vertical line drawn through a grapheme. Sometimes added to distinguish one grapheme | from another.

Barcelona chair, the is a chair designed by Ludwig Mies van der Rohe and Lilly Reich in 1929. The form is said to be inspired by Roman folding chairs known as the Curule chair. The Barcelona Chair is still produced by Knoll International.

Barcode The first barcode was read on a ten-pack of Wrigley's.

Barnack, Oskar The father of the Leica was forced by medical condition to design the first ever light-weight camera. Because Barnack suffered from asthma he was unable to carry heavy tripod-mounted cameras. In 1913 he developed the original Leica.

Barcelona Chair, 1929 (above). Design: Ludwig Mies van der Rohe and Lilly Reich. Curule chair, 1870 (below). © Knoll International.

Barnbrook, Jonathan is a British graphic designer, film maker and typographer. In 2001 Barnbrook created a design entitled "Designers, stay away from corporations that want you to lie for them", a quote from Tibor Kalman which was used on a large-format advertising billboard.

Oskar Barnack and the original Leica. © Leica Camera AG.

Base

Baseline.

Baseline The invisible line where letters sit.
Baseline Magazine is a Magazine about typography and graphic design and is characterized by its large format.
Baskerville, John was a noted English type designer and printer. In honour of his work, the local artist David Patten created a Portland stone sculpture of the Baskerville typeface in front of Baskerville's House in Centenary Square, Birmingham. The sculptural tribute "Industry and Genius" is probably the world's only civic monument to a typeface.
Bass, Saul was a graphic designer and Academy Award winning filmmaker, best known for his design of motion picture title sequences, film posters, and corporate logos. In

1974, Saul Bass directed his only feature-length science-fiction film, called Phase IV.
Bastard type having the face of a larger or smaller size than the actual body text.

universal
abcdefghijklmnopqrstuvwxyz

Herbert Bayer's experimental universal typeface, 1925.

Bayer, Herbert was an Austrian and American graphic designer, painter, photographer, sculptor, interior designer, and architect, who was widely recognized as the last living member of the Bauhaus. Herbert Bayer was also an advocate of the "New Typography" that proclaimed to only use lower case letters. This fact concluded in Bayer's experimental typeface, named universal.

Poster Design by Lester Beall for the Rural Electrification Administration, 1934.

Beall, Lester was one of the leading proponent of modernist graphic design in the United States. Beall's 1939 photomontage poster promoting the Rural Electrification Administration's campaign is considered to be one of the greatest American posters of all time and was sold at an auction for a record price of $38,400.

Beck, Henry Charles also known as Harry Beck is most famous for creating the London Underground Tube map in 1931. In his spare time he hand-lettered more than 2,400 characters in Railway Type.

Inscription on the entrance of the Reichstag in Berlin. © Lighttracer.

Behrens, Peter was a noted architect and designer (1968–1949) who obtained permission for designing the inscription on the entrance of the German Reichstag in Berlin "Dem Deutschen Volke" (To the German People). Behrens utilized a font which he had created for a catalogue on the German contributions to the World Exhibition in St. Louis. In cooperation with the female designer Anna Simons he produced the inscription as early as 1908.

Bel Geddes, Norman was a theatrical and industrial designer who became a pioneer in creating futur-

istic concepts like a 9-deck amphibian airliner, an Art Deco House of Tomorrow or a teardrop-shaped automobile.

Model of teardrop-shaped automobile Design: Bel Geddes. © A. Van Dyke.

Bell Centennial is a sans-serif typeface designed by Matthew Carter. Bell Centennial was commissioned by AT&T to replace their current typeface Bell Gothic. They needed a typeface that would fit more characters per line on a single page of a phone book without the loss of legibility. Carter increased the x-height of lowercase characters, condensed the character width, and drew the letters with deep ink traps, designed to fill in ink due to high-speed printing on common newsprint paper.

ABCDEFGHIJKLMNO
PQRSTUVWXYZÀÅÉÎ
ÕÜabcdefghijklmnop
qrstuvwxyzàåéîõü
&1234567890($£.,!?)

Bell Centennial by Matthew Carter.

Bellini, Carlo is an Italian product designer best known for his lamp

"Eddy", a rare light with flexible limbs that can be shaped into any position.

Eddy, 1985. Design: Carlo Bellini.
© ETOZ / M. Reitmeier.

Benguiat, Ed is actually a qualified drummer. Under the pseudonym "Eddie Benart" he played with famous musicians like Stan Kenton and Woody Herman.

Bennett, Ward was an American designer, artist and sculptor who is considered to be one of the first designers to use industrial design in home design. Ward had a strong interest in chair design because he had back problems of his own. He had designed over 100 chairs by 1979.

Bensistor, the is a tonal-poem generator, designed to inspire to play with words, syllables and sounds. It was invented by Harald Taglinger, who wanted to pay homage to the philosopher and theorist of design Max Bense. The idea was to have scraps of conversation form possible sound structures and patterns of words.

Bentley Max Bill's preferred brand of car was a Bentley with the Zurich License Plate ZH–97 97. He proclaimed that everyone should be driving a Bentley.

Benton, Morris Fuller was an influential American typeface designer who completed an unbelievable amount of 221 typefaces, including ATF Bodoni, Goudy Old Style, Cheltenham, Bank Gothic, Franklin Gothic, Broadway and many more.

Berliner is a popular page size for newspapers, measuring 315 × 470 mm. It is also called "midi".

Berners-Lee, Tim is a British scientist at CERN, who invented the World Wide Web (WWW) in 1989. The web was originally conceived and developed to meet the demand for automatic information-sharing between scientists in universities and institutes around the world.

Bernhard, Lucian was a German graphic and type designer during the first half of the twentieth century. He was influential in helping create the design style known as "Plakatstil" and became the first professor for poster design at the "Academy of Fine Arts" in 1920.

Bertoia, Harry was an Italian-born American furniture designer and sound art sculptor. Bertoia started his career designing jewellery and even created wedding rings for the well-known Ray and Charles Eames.

Bevel A tool in design software for drawing angles or modifying the surface of your work to a certain inclination.

Bézier Curve A parametric curve that represents a vector path. They are drawn using a pen tool and by placing anchor points which can be controlled to form shapes or lines.

Biáng is one of the most complex Chinese characters in contemporary usage. It is made up of 58 strokes in its traditional form (43 strokes in simplified Chinese).

The character for Biáng in calligraphic regular script.

Bible The Bible has been printed in at least 275 languages.

Sticker "Ein Herz für Kinder" (A heart for children). Design: Willy Fleckhaus.

Bild The daily German newspaper once persuaded Willy Fleckhaus to act as an Art Director. It was for the design of the sticker "Ein Herz für Kinder".

Billboard Large format outdoor advertising, usually placed in high traffic areas.

Bill, Max was a Swiss architect, artist, designer and representative of the Zurich School of Concrete. From 1924–1927 his creative work began when he made an apprenticeship as a silver smith at the "Kunstgewerbeschule" in Zurich. It is less known that two years later he was expelled from school due to lateness and showing up in a carnival costume.

Biomorphism is an Art movement that focuses on the power of natural life and uses organic shapes.

Biomorphism inspired a lot of famous designers like Marc Newson, Isamo Noguchi and Alvar Aalto. The term was first coined in 1935.

Biomorphic Spacelander Bicycle, 1946. Design: Benjamin G. Bowden. © Brooklyn Museum.

Bi Sheng was the Chinese inventor of the first known movable type technology. Bi Sheng's system was made of Chinese porcelain and was invented between 1041 and 1048 during the Song dynasty, 400 years earlier than Johannes Gutenberg invented his printing process.

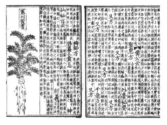

The Bencao on traditional Chinese medicine. Printed with a woodblock printing press in 1249.

Bit Abbreviation for BInary digiT. A bit is either 1, meaning "on" or 0, meaning "off". A sequence of 8 bits describe 1 byte which for example can contain actual characters or colour information.

Bitmap A series of bits that forms a structure representing a graphic image. The colour of each pixel is individually defined.

BITSTREAM®

Bitstream Inc. logo.

Bitstream Inc. was the first type foundry dedicated entirely to digital type. It was founded by Matthew Carter and Mike Parker in 1981.

Black Flag Logo, 1976. Design: Raymond Ginn.

Black Flag was an American punk rock band formed in 1976. Their minimalist logo was as brutal and uncompromising as their sound. The strong four-bar design by Raymond Ginn was a hit amongst Los Angeles teens, who made it popular in the graffiti scene. The logo was inspired by the reversal of a white flag.

Blackletter

Blackletter, also known as Gothic script, Gothic minuscule, or Textura.

Blackletter was a Gothic script used throughout Western Europe from the 12th to the 15th century for copying manuscripts and in certain early printing processes. It continued to be used for the German language until the 20th century.

Blackspot Sneaker, 2004. © Adbusters.

Blackspot Sneaker, the is a sneaker produced by Adbusters, an anticonsumption organization, founded in Canada. It comes in black or red and features a 100% organic hemp upper and hand drawn logo (the so called anti-logo). The Blackspot Sneaker should serve as an example to prove that running an ethical, environmentally responsible business is possible.

Blase, Karl-Oskar Blase is not only known for his stamp design and being the graphical director for documenta, he also erected his own monument during his lifetime. The monument is over two

meters high in the shape of an eye erected to himself in the nature park Habichtswald in Kassel, Germany.

Bleed Describes a certain area to be trimmed off. It gives the printer a small amount of space to account for movement of the paper, and design inconsistencies. After trimming, the bleed ensures that no unprinted edges occur in the final trimmed document. Bleeds in the US generally are 1/8 of an inch from where the cut is to be made. Bleeds in the UK and Europe generally are 2 to 5 mm.

Bley, Thomas S. was the only German designer in the famous Memphis Group. In the early 1980s he designed a chair and a triangular side-table featuring the characteristic Memphis-look.

Blind embossed business cards.

Blind de/embossing A print process that does not include the use of ink or foil to highlight a design. An embossed pattern is raised against the background, while a debossed pattern is sunken into the surface.

Blind folio A page number that is not printed on the page.

Block quotation A block quotation is a quotation in a written docu-

ment, that is set apart in order to clearly distinguish it from the main text usually set in a different typeface or smaller size font.

Blow is the name of the first mass-produced inflatable chair, designed by the Italian product designers De Pas, D'Urbino, and Lomazzi in 1960.

Blueline A monochrome proof that is generated from film and used to check the layout and positioning of pages on a signature. The blue colour was originally chosen to prevent reproduction.

Bluffalo Bill was the nickname Ferdinand Kramer made up for his colleague Max Bill.

Blurb A comment from a review (often by another author praising a particular book) printed on the dust wrapper or on a wrap-around band.

FF Blur

FF Blur typeface, 1992. Design: Neville Brody.

Blur The eroded typeface FF Blur, designed by Neville Brody is made by using a Helvetica or Akzidenz Grotesk that he put through Adobe Photoshop's blur filter.

BMW Culture Book, the is probably the first book that features an integrated, remote-controlled engine and can be driven around. The book, containing cultural activities of BMW, is limited to 1488 hand-signed copies and was designed by Stefan Sagmeister in 2011.

Boards Thin pieces of wood, generally covered in leather, that were attached to the assembled printed pages to form the binding.

Bodoni, Giambattista was an Italian typographer, type designer and printer. In his life Bodoni designed and personally engraved 298 typefaces and managed to produce roughly 1,200 fine editions. With good reason he is called the "King of typographer".

Body type is the term for the text forming the main content of a book, magazine, web page or other printed matter.

Bofinger chair, the was the first one-piece plastic chair worldwide in fibreglass-reinforced polyester to be mass-produced in one single pressing process. The Bofinger Chair, also named BA 1171, was designed by German architect and designer Helmut Bätzner in close co-operation with Bofinger company in 1964.

Bofinger chair, 1964. Design: Helmut Bätzner.

Book formats (cm)

miniature	Less than 5 × 4
sexagesimo-quarto	5 × 7.5
quadragesimo-octavo	6.5 × 10
tricesimo-secondo	9 × 14
octodecimo	10 × 16.5
sextodecimo	10 × 17
duodecimo	12.5 × 19
duodecimo (large)	14 × 18
crown octavo	13.5 × 20
octavo	15 × 23
medium octavo	16.5 × 23.5
royal octavo	16.5 × 25
super octavo	18 × 28
imperial octavo	21 × 29
quarto	24 × 30.5
folio	30.5 × 48
elephant folio	58.5 to 63.5
atlas folio	63.5 to 127
double elephant folio	127 +

Book of Kells is an illuminated manuscript Gospel book in Latin, containing the four Gospels of the New Testament together with various prefatory texts and tables. It is a masterwork of Western calligraphy. It is also regarded as Ireland's finest national treasure.

Book of Kells: Folio 27 from the Lindisfarne Gospels.

Boom, Irma is a Dutch graphic designer, who specializes in book making. She has often been specified as the "The Queen of Books". She created more than 300 books for clients like the Rijksmuseum in Amsterdam, The Museum of Modern Art New York and the Fondazione Prada.

Border The decorative design or edge of a surface, line, or area that forms it's outer boundary.

Bormann Decree, the issued by Martin Bormann in 1941 under orders of Adolf Hitler banning the use of Fraktur, claiming it to be of Jewish origin. Ironically the Germans used Fraktur type on the letterhead.

Boros, Christian In 2003 the German advertiser Christian Boros bought a bunker in Berlin to present its art collection. The collection focuses on artists of his generation.

Bouma In typography, a Bouma is the shape of a cluster of letters, often a whole word. The term "Bouma-shape", which was probably first used in Paul Saenger's 1997 book "Space between Words" has its origin in reference to hypotheses by prominent vision researcher Herman Bouma, who studied the shapes and confusability of letters and letter strings. Some typographers have believed that, when reading, people recognize words by deciphering Boumas, not just individual letters, or that the shape of the word is related to readability and/or legibility.

Ear

Bowl.

Bowl A curved stroke that encloses a letter's counter.

BP logo by AR Saunders, 1920.

BP The British multinational oil and gas company had its first logo made by Mr. AR Saunders from the purchasing department. Saunders won an employee competition in 1920 to design the first BP mark. It showed the letters B and P with wings on their edges, set into the outline of a shield.

Bracket A bracket is a tall punctuation mark typically used in matched pairs within text, to set apart or interject other text. Used unqualified, brackets refer to different types of brackets in different parts of the world and in different contexts. Brackets include round brackets/parentheses, square brackets, curly brackets, angle brackets, and various other pairs of symbols.

Braille alphabet, 1821.

Braille, Louis was a French inventor of a system of reading and writing for use by the blind or visually impaired. His system, developed in 1821, remains known worldwide as braille. The braille alphabet uses 6-dot cells to create readable characters.

Branding The process involved in creating a unique name and image for a product in the consumers' mind, primarily through advertising campaigns with a consistent theme.

Brandt, Marianne was a German painter, graphic designer, sculptor, and photographer who studied at the Bauhaus school and became head of the metal workshop in 1928. Today, Brandt's designs for household objects such as lamps, ashtrays and teapots are considered the harbinger of modern industrial design.

Broadsheet Describes the largest format that is used for printing newspapers. The full broadsheet spread measures 59.6 × 74.9 cm.

Brodovitch, Alexey is a legend in graphic design. His use of assymetrical layouts, white space and dynamic imagery changed the nature of editorial design. He was responsible for commissioning work from cutting-edge artists such as Cassandre, Dalí, Cartier-Bresson, and Man Ray.

Hamburgefons

Industria Solid typeface, 1989. Design: Neville Brody.

Brody, Neville is an English designer, typographer and art director, most known for his work on The Face magazine and for designing record covers for bands like Cabaret Voltaire or Depeche Mode.

Less known is that he was almost thrown out of college because he put the Queen's head sideways on a postage stamp design.

Brownjohn, Robert was an American graphic designer who is best known for his James Bond title sequences, especially for "From Russia with Love" and "Goldfinger", where he used the technique of projecting moving footage onto the bodies of models.

Structure of the Buckminsterfullerene.

Buckyballs The spherical arrangements, which permit the creation of new materials and allow for new functions, were named fullerenes in honour of Richard Buckminster Fuller. Non-oblate fullerenes are also referred to as "buckyballs".

Bullet A bullet is a typographical symbol (•) or glyph used to introduce items in a list.

Bulls Eye A spot or imperfection in printing caused by dirt or hardened specks of ink. The problem is most visible in areas of heavy ink coverage.

Burri, René was a Swiss photographer who is famous for portraits of Pablo Picasso and Che Guevara.

The images of Guevara smoking a cigar have become some of the most iconic photographs ever made.

"Work hard and be nice to people".
Design: Anthony Burrill. © mia!

Burrill, Anthony is a British graphic artist and print-maker. His famous and hundred times copied letterpress print titled "Work hard & be nice to People" was inspired by a conversation he eavesdropped in a local supermarket. An old lady was sharing the wise words to the checkout girl.

Buzzword A buzzword is a word or phrase that becomes very popular for a period of time. The term was first used in 1946 as student slang.

BYGMCR Short for BuY General Motors CaRs: a simple rule to remind you about the complimentary colours: Blue versus Yellow, Green versus Magenta and Cyan versus Red.

Byline A line added to an article to identify its author(s), especially in magazine and newspaper publishing.

Byrne, David The singer of the Pop group Talking Heads, whose LP's were designed by Tibor Kalman and later on by Stefan Sagmeister, was a designer himself. Byrne studied at the Rhode Island School of Design.

C

Boomerang desk, 1969.
Design: Maurice Calka. © Serge Calka.

Calka, Maurice was a polish sculptor and designer who achieved worldwide recognition because of his "Boomerang desk", a molded fiberglass desk, designed at the end of the sixties.

Calkins, Ernest Elmo was a deaf American advertising pioneer who introduced the use of art and fictional characters in advertising. He has been called the "Dean of Advertising Men".

Camel As a template for the cigarette manufacturers logo served an old dromedary from the circus Barum & Bailey, who just guested in the city.

Cantilever chair, the is one of the landmark achievements of avantgarde furniture design of the 20s. The special thing about it is without a doubt its floating back and his L-shape serving as the chair's supporting base.

Capote, Truman The famous writer basically only wrote on yellow paper.

Care Package The care packages the US parachuted into Afghanistan in 2001 had the same colour as the splinter bombs US planes had scattered only a little earlier, namely yellow. Air Force thereupon announced that the colour of

the packages was changed to blue.

Carson, David In 1980, professional surfer Carson attented a three-week type workshop in Rapperswil run by Hans-Rudolf Lutz. Today, the self-taught Graphic designer still considers Lutz (1939–1998) to have influenced him the most.

Casino by Martin Scorsese was the last movie Saul Bass, an American graphic designer, created a movie title sequence before he unfortunately passed away in 1996.

W CASLON JUNR

Two Line English Egyptian, first ever printed sans serif.

Caslon, William In 1816, William Caslon IV produced the first ever sans-serif printing type in England for Latin characters under the title "Two Lines English Egyptian".

Yves Saint Laurent logo, 1961.
Design: A.M. Cassandre.

Cassandre, A. M. was a French-Ukrainian commercial poster artist, and typeface designer. In 1961, he designed the well-known Yves Saint Laurent logo and is also responsible for various typefaces, including the famous Peignot.

Caxton, William is considered to be the first English person to introduce a printing press into England, which he did in 1476. He was also the first English retailer of printed books.

CBS logo, 1950.

CBS It is said that the inspiration for the CBS "eye" logo, came from Pennsylvania Dutch folk art painted on their barns to ward off evil. The logo was designed by William Golden in 1950.

CC The CC in emails stands for "Carbon Copy".

CD-ROM The hole in the middle of a CD-ROM has its origins in the size of an Old Dutch 10-cent coin. That item was the only thing the developers of Philips constantly had in their purses. The size of the diameter of the coin seemed to be ideal for the application.

Century Guild, the greatly influenced the Arts & Crafts movement of the late 1800s. It was established by Arthur Mackmurdo, a progressive English architect and designer, in 1882.

Chair Thing, the is from a series of pieces named "Stool Thing" and "Table Thing", all designed by the British designer Peter Murdoch. Murdoch's designs were mass-produced and approximately 76,000

pieces were sold over a six-month period in 1967. The "Chair Thing" is designed especially for children and is made from a single piece of folded cardboard.

The "Chair Thing" by Peter Murdoch.

Chaise Longue LC4 The renowned Chaise Longue created by Le Corbusier, Pierre Jeanneret and Charlotte Perriand is actually inspired by American Cowboys who, after hard day's work, sit down in chairs on a veranda, tilt the backs back, stretch out their legs and rest their boots on the balustrade.

Chaise Longue LC4, 1928. © Cassina.

Chalet In 1996, House Industries, a type foundry and design studio from Yorklyn, released the plain geometric sans serif typeface Chalet. To promote the new release they made up the fictional character René Albert Chalet and named him as the creator. From then on it became a big success.

Chanel

Chanel logo.

Flywheel, 1992, released by FontHaus.
Design: Christian Schwartz.

Chanel In the early 1920s, the famous Coco Chanel finally was allowed to use Château de Crémat's double-C logo for her own brand.

Chicago

Chicago, 1983. Design: Susan Kare.

Chicago is the name of the bit-mapped screen font to be used on the first Apple Macintosh operating system. It was created by Susan Kare in 1983.

Chinese The Chinese language is composed entirely of pictograms. It contains over 80,000 of them – although only 3,500 are most commonly used.

Chinese pictogram for "Love".

Chip Kidd is an American graphic designer, best known for his innovative book covers. Charles Kidd, got his nickname "Chip" from his mother before he was even born.

Christian Schwartz The popular type designer released his first commercially available typeface at the age of 14! It was called Flywheel.

Chroma The attribute of colour that specifies the amount of saturation or strength. This term is mainly used in accordance to the Munsell colour space model.

Chruxin, Christian The German typography and graphic artist was one of the creators of the systematically oriented Kassel school of poster art, book and magazine design. Chruxin died early at the age of 69 years. On his grave stands a briefcase with the inscription "passes from 17 o'clock".

Chupa Chups logo, 1969. © Salvador Dalí.

Chupa Chups In 1969 it is believed that Dalí was approached by Spanish confectioners Chupa Chups to design a new logo, and the result became as instantly recognisable as his melting clocks. Dalí incorporated the Chupa Chups name into a brightly coloured daisy shape. Always keenly aware of branding, Dalí suggested that the logo be placed on top of the lolly instead of the side so that it could always be seen intact.

Chwast, Seymour is an American graphic designer, illustrator, type designer and part of the Push Pin Studios, now The Pushpin Group, Inc. in New York City. Chwast is famous for his commercial artwork, which includes posters, food packaging and magazine covers. In 1979, he was hired by McDonald's to design the first box for their Happy Meals.

Cicero A cicero is a unit of measure used in typography in Italy, France and other continental European countries, first used by Pannartz and Sweynheim in 1468 for the edition of Cicero's Epistles, Ad Familiares. The font size thus acquired the name cicero. It is 1/6 of the historical French inch, and is divided into 12 points, known in English as French points or Didot points. The unit of the cicero is similar to an English pica, although the French inch was slightly larger than the English inch. There are about 1.063 picas to a cicero; a pica is 4.23333333 mm and a cicero is 4.5 mm.

Circumflex A diacritical mark (â) placed above a vowel in some languages to indicate a special phonetic quality.

Clarendon is considered the first registered typeface in 1845. Clarendon is a slab-serif typeface that was created by Robert Besley for Thorowgood and Co., a letter foundry known as the Fann Street Foundry. The typeface was appar-ently named after the Clarendon Press in Oxford.

Clarendon

abcdefghijklmnopqrstuvwxyz 1234567890!@#$%^&*()

Clarendon typeface. Design: Robert Besley.

Clipart Ready-made artwork, like illustrations, symbols, graphics, sold or distributed for clipping and pasting.

CMYK Stands for Cyan, Magenta, Yellow, and Key colour. This colour model also called process colour, is a subtractive colour model used in colour printing.

Coated Paper Coating restricts the amount of ink that is absorbed by the paper and how the ink bleeds into the paper. Especially suited for sharp and complex images as the ink stays on top of the paper.

Coca-Cola logo set in Spencerian Script.

Coca-Cola The Coca-Cola logo was created by Platt Rogers Spencer and first published in the late 19th century. It was made using a style of hand lettering called Spencerian Script.

Codex is a book constructed of a number of sheets of paper or papyrus with hand-written contents. It replaced the scroll and has been called the most important precursor of a bound and printed book as we know today.

Coffins Two well-known designers even designed coffins: Luigi Colani and Egon Eiermann.

Coiner, Charles Toucey was an American painter and advertising art director. He was the first known person who commissioned works from modern artists such as Salvador Dalí and Pablo Picasso. In 1964, Coiner became the first American given the Art Director's Award of Distinction.

Colani A Colani is a dark-blue sailor jacket that was manufactured by the tailor's shop Berger & Colani. Mr. Colani who was co-owner of the shop was a forebear of Luigi Colani, the well-known German product designer.

Colani GT In 1975 Jochen Feldhusen from Gelsenkirchen purchased a Colani GT, the legendary ultra-flat roadster which the master designer Luigi Colani developed on the basis of a VW Beetle platform and ever since admirers have been flocking to see the chassis. Once a year the GT fans get together for a grand drive-out.

Collins, Brian became the first graphic designer to held a lecture about communication and design at the World Economic Forum held in Switzerland.

Collotype A printing process employing a glass plate with a gelatin surface that carries the image to be reproduced. It was invented by Alphonse Poitevin in 1856.

Colombo, Joe was one of the most radical Italian industrial designer. Since the beginning of his career in the 1950s Colombo was most interested in ever-changing living systems. The two best examples of these "dynamic pieces of furniture" were the 1963 "Mini-kitchen" and the 1971 "Total Furnishing Unit" which presented a complete "living-machine" including a modular Kitchen, Cupboard, Bed and Bathroom.

Joe Colombo, Total Furnishing Unit, 1971. © Joe Colombo.

Colophon A printed or handwritten statement at the end of a book, providing details about its production, the print run, the name of the printer, the paper used, the typefaces used, and the date of printing.

Colour Blindness affects a large number of individuals, with protanopia and deuteranopia being the most common types. In individuals with Northern European ancestry, as many as 8 % of men and 0.4 % of women experience congenital colour deficiency.

Compasso d'Oro was the first european industrial design award of its kind, originated in Italy in 1954. Famous award winners were Achille Castiglioni, Bruno Munari, Richard Sapper, Mario Bellini and many more.

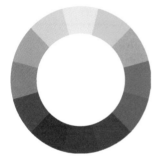

The logo of the Compasso d'Oro, depicting a compass to measure the Golden Section. © ADI Design.

Complementary Colours Colours that are opposite of each other when viewed on the colour wheel.

Traditional colour wheel.

Composing stick In letterpress and typesetting, a composing stick is a tool used to assemble pieces of metal type into words and lines, which are then transferred to a galley before being locked into a form and printed. Early composing sticks were made of wood, but later iron, brass, steel, aluminium, pewter and other metals were used.

Condensed Type A narrow, elongated typeface in which the set-widths of the characters is narrower than in the standard typeface.

Cooper Black

Cooper Black typeface, 1920. Design: Oswald B. Cooper.

Cooper, Oswald B. was an American type and graphic designer who created the famous Cooper Black typeface in 1920. In early 1930, Cooper attempted to protect his successful font by means of a patent. In 1931 a judge ruled that some of the Cooper Black characters had been taken from a brand logo known prior to 1920. The first attempt to protect the form of a typeface failed.

Cooper Union logo. Design: Herb Lubalin.

Cooper Union is one of the nation's oldest institutions of higher learning, dedicated exclusively to preparing students for the professions of art, architecture and engineering. Graduates of the Cooper Union School of Art include Seymour Chwast, Lou Dorfsman, Milton Glaser, and Herb Lubalin.

Cornelius The rooster on the Kellogg's Corn Flakes packaging is called Cornelius.

The rooster Cornelius. © Kellogg's.

Counter Fully or partially enclosed space within a letter.

Courier is a monospaced slab serif typeface, made by Howard "Bud" Kettler in 1955. All characters have the same width, which makes it practical for all kinds of documents, e.g. invoices. Courier was actually called Messenger. Here is what Howard Kettler said about the name change: "A letter can be just an ordinary messenger, or it can be the courier, which radiates dignity, prestige, and stability." Courier was later redrawn by Adrian Frutiger for the IBM Selectric Composer series of electric typewriters.

Courier

Courier Typeface, 1955. Design: Howard Kettler.

Cranbrook Academy of Art, the is a leading graduate school of architecture, art and design, formed in 1932 in the US. Notable alumni include Harry Bertoia, Charles and Ray Eames, Florence Knoll, Daniel Libeskind and Eero Saarinen.

Crasset, Matali is a French industrial designer that turned her haircut into a logo.

Crossbar A crossbar is a horizontal stroke.

Crouwel, Wim was obsessed with grids. This fact earned him the nickname "Gridnik" or "Mr. Gridnik".

Matali Crasset's logotype. Design: Sebastien Dragon.

Culture Jamming is an intriguing form of political communication that has emerged in response to the commercial isolation of public life. The term "cultural jamming" and the concept behind it first appeared on JamCon'84, a cassette-only release by the audio-collage band called "Negativland".

Crossbar.

Cursive also known as script is a typeface representational of handwriting.

Curtis, David Hillman was a popular American author, musician and filmmaker. In 1996, while working as a design director at Macromedia, he designed the first website using new technology, a browser plug-in called Flash, which became a milestone in Web Design. Glide magazine actually called him the "Michael Jordan of web design".

Cuts In the world of letterpress, stock images are called cuts. These black and white images were the first illustrations on relief presses, before photography and offset printing was used in Newspaper Ads.

More free downloadable Cuts are available on www.briarpress.org.

Cut-up technique The cut-up technique (or découpé in French) is an aleatory literary technique in which a text is cut up and rearranged to create a new text. The concept can be traced to at least the Dadaists of the 1920s, but was popularized in the late 1950s and early 1960s by writer William S. Burroughs, and has since been used in a wide variety of contexts.

Cyan is one of the primary colours, along with magenta, yellow, and black. Cyan is also called process blue.

Cyberspace William Gibson created the term "Cyberspace" in his novel "Neuromancer" in 1984.

Dagger

Dymaxion car

Dagger A footnote reference that is used after the asterisk.

"WORK. THINK. FEEL."

Advice from Louis Danziger to his students.

USS West Mahomet in dazzle camouflage, 1918.

Danziger, Louis Once a publisher asked Lou Danziger to give advice to art students. He answered: "Work. Think. Feel." Work: "No matter how brilliant, talented, exceptional, and wonderful the student may be, without work there is nothing but potential and talk." Think: "Design is a problem-solving activity. Thinking is the application of intelligence to arrive at the appropriate solution to the problem." Feel: "Work without feeling, intuition, and spontaneity is devoid of humanity."

Dazzle camouflage also known as razzle dazzle or dazzle painting, which applied colour and geometrics on navy ships used extensively in World War I. The pioneer of this movement was Norman Wilkinson, a British marine artist.
De Bono, Edward is a Maltese physician, psychologist and author. He is named as a huge inspiration for the work by Stefan Sagmeister, who uses one of de Bonos method that suggests starting to think about an idea for a particular project by taking a random object as point of departure.

"Dauphine" desktop calculator, 1997. Design: George Sowden. © Alessi.

Dauphine is the name of a desktop calculator, designed by George Sowden in the 1990s. It was especially made for the kitchen with its rounded body and buttons.

Abc

The typeface Caslon, 1722.

Declaration of Independence The first copies of the US Declaration of Independence were printed in Caslon, a font designed by William Caslon in 1722.
Decorative line Typographic term for a shaped line, which is characterized by the fact that it is fine at

the ends and the centre becomes thicker. There are different shapes that can be assigned to different style epochs, such as Art Nouveau or Art Deco.

Denotation is a translation of a sign to its meaning, precisely to its literal meaning, more or less like dictionaries try to define it. Denotation is sometimes contrasted to connotation, which translates a sign to meanings associated with it.

Descender.

Descender A downward vertical stroke found on lowercase letters that extends below the baseline.

Design Award The only design award which was awarded only once is the award for "lovely, crinkly edges". In Douglas Adams novel "The Hitchhiker's Guide to the Galaxy", the plant designer Slartibartfast gets an award for designing the coast of Norway.

Designers Republic, the is a graphic design studio based in Sheffield, England, founded in 1986 by Ian Anderson and Nick Phillips. They are probably best known for their in-game artwork, packaging and manual for The Wipeout video game series.

Design for the real world is a book by Victor J. Papanek, published in 1970. The book contains his own and his student's work, which challenges the industrial design establishment to design for the handicapped and disadvantaged. The book was translated and published in 23 languages and is probably the most widely read book on design.

the DESIGN MUSEUM

Logo of the Design Museum.

Design Museum, the is currently housed in a former 1940s banana warehouse on the south bank of the River Thames. The Museum opened its doors in 1989 and attracts 200,000 visitors annually.

Design Revue Marcus Botsch and Winfried Scheuer released a satire publication, entitled "Design Revue" that enduringly shattered the design community – and created a great deal of amusement.

De Stijl Magazine, 1928.

De Stijl was a Dutch artistic movement founded in 1917 in Amsterdam. It is also known as neoplasticism and was characterised by abstraction and reduction to the essentials of form and colour. De Stijl, Dutch for "The Style" was also the name of a magazine published from 1917–1920 by Theo van Doesburg.

Devanagari Script.

Devanagari also called Nagari is an alphabet of India and Nepal that is written from left to right and lacks distinct letter cases. The top of all the characters are connected by a horizontal line. It has a strong preference for symmetrical rounded shapes within squared outlines. Devanagari is a script based on syllables, meaning the smallest unit is the syllable, not the letter. Devanagari is used for over 120 languages, including Hindi, Marathi, Nepali, Sanskrit etc.

Diacritical marks: Accent acute, cedille and circumflex.

De Vinne, Theodore Low was a late 19th century American printer, typographer and an important scholarly author on typography. He was also one of nine men who founded the Grolier Club in January 1884. It is the oldest existing bibliophilic club in North America.
Diacritic A diacritical mark, point or sign added to a letter or character to give it a particular phonetic value. Examples are the cedilla, tilde, circumflex and macron.

Diagonal Stroke.

Diagonal Stroke An angled stroke.

Frontispiece of the Chinese Diamond Sutra, the oldest known dated printed book in the world.

Diamond Sutra The Diamond Sutra is, according to the British Library, "the earliest complete survival of a dated printed book."
Dictionary The Japanese have the largest dictionary of over 500,000 words, this includes foreign loan words, neologisms, archaisms, idiomatic phrases, Chinese characterisations and slang. Followed by the Dutch with 430,000 words.

Didone The term Didone is a melding of the two typefaces Didot and Bodoni. Didone typefaces (also referred to as Neoclassical and Modern) are characterized by extreme weight contrast between thicks and thins, vertical stress, and serifs with little or no bracketing.

Firmin Didot (1764–1836).

Didot, Firmin Francois' son, along with Giambattista Bodoni, was one of the typographers responsible for the development of the Didone, a serif typeface which is characterized by high contrast of strokes and hairline serifs.

Didot, François-Ambroise was a French publisher and book printer. In 1780 he adapted Fournier's point system for sizing typefaces by width, using units of 1/72 of the pre-metric French inch. The Didot point, named after him, has been mostly replaced by the DTP point in Europe and throughout the world.

Die Cut is a die that cut shapes or holes in different materials to make the design stand out.

Diffrient, Niels was an American industrial designer. In 2007, the famous Forbes magazine named Diffrient the "granddaddy of the ergonomic revolution".

Digi Grotesk

Digi Grotesk, Hell Design Studio, 1968.

Digi Grotesk is said to be one of the earliest digital fonts ever created. It was designed in 1968 by the Hell Design Studio and was available in seven weights from light to bold.

Digiset was the first typesetting machine that worked with digitally assembled typefaces. It was created by German inventor Dr. Rudolf Hell in 1966.

Digital The word digital is derived from the Latin word Digitus, which means "finger".

Digraph Two regular characters to which one sound is applied, e.g., "ph" in English is pronounced "f".

Diminuendo Irish monks developed the principle of diminuendo which applied diminishing scale to typography on a page.

FF DIN on a German street sign, 1995. Design: Albert-Jan Pool.

DIN 1451 is a sans-serif typeface that is widely used for German traffic, and technical applications. For decades, the DIN typeface was considered to be a creation without a real creator. But researches have shown that the Siemens engineer Ludwig Goller (1884–1964) was responsible, as chairman of the DIN committee for design, for the development of the typeface, which is actually based on hand lettering that go back to 1905, when the Royal Prussian Railway Administration used it on all its rolling stock. In 1995 Albert-Jan Pool started to design FF DIN, focused on improved readability.

Various Dingbats.

Dingbat An ornament used in typesetting to add space around an image or a symbol. Some fonts like Zapf Dingbats only contain symbols.

Diphthong A speech sound that, within one syllable, changes from one vowel sound to another.

Dogcow The Dogcow, also known as Clarus the Dogcow is a mysterious animal that looked like a mixture between a dog and a cow and that lived on the Page Setup screen of Macintosh computers. It was originally created in 1983 as

part of the Cairo font by Susan Kare as the glyph for "z".

Dogcow. © Apple Inc.

Dog Ear A dog ear is a phrase that refers to the folded down corner of a page that can serve as a bookmark.

Dog Lamp The New York-based graphic duo Hjalti Karlsson and Jan Wilker created the iconic Dog Lamp which depicts the body of a plastic dog that sticks up out of the lampshade. The shade is strongly reminiscent of one of those protective collars round sick dogs to prevent them scratching.

Domains

ac	Ascension Island
aw	Aruba
bf	Burkina Faso
bi	Benin
bv	Bouvet Island
cx	Christmas Island
fi	Fiji
gp	Guadeloupe
ht	Haiti
im	Isle of Man, the
is	Iceland
kz	Kazakhstan
lv	Latvia
mc	Monaco
no	Norway
om	Oman
sh	St. Helena
tg	Togo
ug	Uganda
va	Vatican
ye	Yemen
za	South Africa

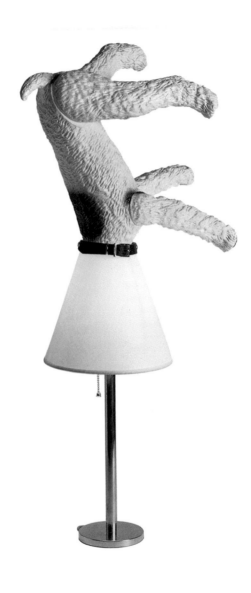

Dot Dot Dot is a magazine of visual culture produced and edited by graphic designers Stuart Bailey and Peter Bil'ak.

Dot Gain When the ink hits the paper, it is absorbed and it somewhat spreads out.

DOT pictograms, the are a set of 50 pictograms. In 1974, the US Department of Transportation (DOT) recognized the need of a standardized visual language for foreign tourists. They commissioned the American Institute of Graphic Arts (AIGA) to produce a comprehensive set of pictograms that can be used by anyone for any purpose, without any licensing issues.

DOT pictograms. Design: Roger Cook and Don Shanosky.

Double Page Spread A double page spread is a layout that extends across two pages.

Double-Truck is a term that refers to a pair of facing pages, usually in a newspaper or magazine with content that stretches over both pages.

Doyle, Christopher The Sydney-based designer has obviously done too many identity projects when he decided to create a set of guidelines for himself, containing colour palettes, clearance space, Do's and Don'ts and so on.

DPI (Dots Per Inch) A term to describe the measure of sharpness within an image.

Tea set, 1879. Design: Christopher Dresser.

Dresser, Christopher was a Scottish designer and design theorist. Associated with the Aesthetic Movement in the second half of the nineteenth century, Dresser is considered the first industrial designer. Some of his metalwork designs are still manufactured by Alessi and Alberto Alessi goes so far as to say Dresser "knew the techniques of metal production better than any designer who has come to Alessi".

Dreyfuss, Henry The US designer cleverly suggested placing weights in alarm clocks he had devised to enhance the impression of great value they conveyed.

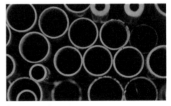

Duotone picture.

Drop Shadow is a visual effect added to an image to give the impression the image is raised above the background by duplicating the shadow.

Dummy A prototype or mock-up of a book, page, or any project designed to resemble and serve as a substitute for the real thing.

Duotone A method of printing an image using two colours, usually black and a spot colour.

Dutch Alphabet The Dutch alphabet consists of 27 letters (a–z and ij).

Dwiggins, William Addison was a well-known American type designer, calligrapher, and book designer. Dwiggins is credited to be the first person coining the term "graphic designer" in 1922.

Dylan, Bob The famous Bob Dylan poster designed by Milton Glaser in 1967 was printed nearly 6 million times and included in slipcovers when the greatest hits album was released.

Dymaxion car, 1933. Design: Buckminster Fuller.

Dymaxion car, the was the provisional prototype of a future car, designed by Buckminster Fuller in the early 1930s. Fuller was aiming for what he called "Omni Medium Transport", an actual vehicle that could go anywhere, even underwater. The word Dymaxion stands for dynamic, maximum, and tension and should summarize his goal to do more with less.

E-13B

Eye

E-13B

E-13B is a font that is optimized for magnetic ink character recognition (MICR), a technique used in the banking industry for processing cheques. There are two major MICR fonts in use: E-13B and CMC-7. E-13B has a 14 character set, while CMC-7 has 15.

1234567890 ⑆ ⑈ ⑇ ⑉

1234567890 ⑆ ⑈ ⑇ ⑉

Above: E-13B, Below: CMC-7.

Eames Lounge Chair When Ray and Charles Eames created their famous Lounge Chair, they had Billy Wilder, the famous filmmaker in their minds, who was given the chair as a birthday present.

Eames, Ray is not only known for his iconic product design, he also designed over half of the covers of "California Arts & Architecture" from 1942 to 1944.

Ear.

Ear A small stroke projecting from the upper right bowl of some lowercase g's.

Edelmann, Heinz was a German illustrator and designer. Between 1961–1969 he was a regular illustrator and cover designer for the internationally renowned magazine twen. He is probably most famous for his art direction and character designs for the 1968 animated film "Yellow Submarine" for the Beatles.

Edition Suhrkamp Collector's Box.
© Suhrkamp Verlag.

Edition Suhrkamp The colouring of the famous paperback series, made by German designer Willy Fleckhaus was inspired by the recently published HKS colour guide.

Inscription at the gates of
Buchenwald concentration camp.
© www.kipomavr.tumblr.com.

Ehrlich, Franz was a German architect who is known for the inscription on the gates of Buchenwald concentration camp. "Jedem das Seine" is a German translation of a Latin phrase that means, "To each what they are due." Ehrlich had trained at the Bauhaus, hated by the Nazis for its internationalism and modernism. The typeface he chose for the sign was a Bauhaus font; the camp authorities either didn't know or didn't care.

Elements of Euclid, the by Greek mathematician Euclid is a mathematical and geometric monograph consisting of 13 books. It was the first innovative book design that used colour rather than labels to teach geometry.

Email The first email was sent in 1969.

Embedding Process of transferring all the data of a font or image into the file itself.

Emboss To give a three-dimensional effect to a text or an image by using highlights and shadows on the sides of the illustration.

Emigre In 1984 Rudy VanderLans launched Emigre magazine which was one of the first publications to use Macintosh computers and which became famous for experimental digital design.

The first emoticon, a smiley, was posted in 1982.

Emoticon The first emoticon, a smiley, was posted in a discussion forum in 1982 by the American Scott E. Fahlmann.

Em space A fixed space equal to the width of the type size being used. The name em was originally a reference to the width of the capital M in the typeface.

English Finish Smooth finish on uncoated book paper.

En space A fixed space equal to one-half of the width of the type size being used.

Engelbart, Douglas invented the world's first computer mouse in 1964. It is made of two gear-wheels positioned perpendicular to each other, allowing movement on one axis. It was mainly made of wood.

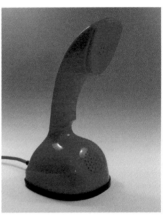

Ericssons Ericofon, 1956. Design: Gösta Thames, Ralph Lysell, and Hugo Blomberg. © Holger Ellgaard.

Engraving To print designs by cutting the surface of a metal plate.

Ephemera is any written or printed matter not meant to be retained or preserved. The word derives from the Greek, meaning "things lasting no more than a day". Some collectible ephemera are advertising trade cards, prospectuses, airsickness bags, bookmarks, catalogues, greeting cards, letters, pamphlets, postcards, posters, defunct stock certificates or tickets, and zines.

EPS is the abbreviation of a graphics file format used to transfer Encapsulated PostScript documents that contain an image, within another PostScript document.

Ericofon, the was the first commercially marketed one-piece telephone. The Ericofon incorporated the dial and handset into a single futuristic looking unit. It was designed in the late 1940s by a team of designers including Gösta Thames, Ralph Lysell, and Hugo Blomberg.

Afri-Cola bottles,1962. © Mineralbrunnen Überkingen-Teinach.

Ernst, Jupp designed the first Afri-Cola bottle as part of a design competition in 1962.

Error 404 The 404 or Not Found error message is a HTTP standard response code indicating that the client was able to communicate with a given server, but the server could not find what was requested. It is named after the server which had its origin in Room 404.

Esquire In 1962, Esquire editor Harold Hayes hired advertising art director George Lois to save the nearly bankrupt magazine. During the 1960s and early 1970s, Lois created 90 covers, an iconic time capsule of politics, graphic design and journalistic dare-devilry, including this cheeky, cutting edge, March 1965 cover on the approaching Women's Movement in America, and the approaching confusion between the sexes.

Esslinger, Hartmut The industrial designer and founder of frog design was candidate for the Green Party in Germany in the 1970s.

Estienne, Robert was one of the most important printers in the 16th century in France. He was the first to print the Bible divided into standard numbered verses.

March 1965 cover of Esquire magazine, a publication of Hearst Communications, Inc. Model: Virna Lisi, Image courtesy: George Lois, Carl Fischer.

Eszett In the German alphabet, the (traditionally lowercase-only) letter ß, called "Eszett", in English "sharp S", is a consonant that evolved as a ligature of "long s and z" and "long s over round s". Since the German orthography reform of 1996, it is used only after long vowels and diphthongs while ss is written after short vowels. The name "Eszett" comes from the two letters s and z as they are pronounced in German.

Etaoin shrdlu is a nonsense phrase that appeared in publications back in the days when Linotype machines were used. To indicate that a line of text was incorrect, the operator pressed all the keys of the first two vertical columns on the left side of the keyboard. Since the letters were arranged by letter frequency, the phrase "etaoinshrdlu" for the English language came up. In other languages, mistakes were indicated by phrases like "esait nrulo" (French), "enis ratulo" (German), "eaosr niltu" (Spanish) and "aeion lrtsu"(Italian).

---o–o---
ETAOIN! SHRDLU! CMFWYP!
New York, July 18.—Here are two reasons why bailiffs, judges, prosecutors and court stenographers die young.
John Ziampettisledibetci was fined $1 for owning an unmuzzled dog.
Robert Tyzyczhowzswiski is asking the court to change his cognomen.

An intentional example of etaoin shrdlu in a 1916 newspaper.

Etch To imprint a design onto the surface of a plate by using a chemical such as acid.

Aluminium replica of "Eternity" at Town Hall Square, Sydney.

Eternity The word Eternity was a graffito tag, that became famous, written over half a million times in the streets of Sydney, Australia.

The word had been tagged by Arthur Stace, a former soldier, in his unmistakable copperplate handwriting. After Stace's death, the Eternity signature lived on and contemporary artist and illustrator Martin Sharp used the tag in many of his works.

Euro currency sign, presented on 12 December 1996.

Euro currency sign It is assumed that the Belgian graphic designer Alain Billiet was the winner of an official competition and thus the designer of the euro sign. The official story of the design history of the euro sign is disputed by Arthur Eisenmenger, a former chief graphic designer for the European Economic Community, who claims he had the idea prior to the European Commission.

Apollo 10 emblem, set in Eurostile. © NASA.

Eurostile The Eurostile type font is a geometric sans-serif typeface designed by Aldo Novarese in 1962. Novarese initially made Eurostile for one of the best-known Italian foundries, Nebiolo, in Turin. It can also be found on the external skin of Apollo 10.

Exclamation mark The English town of Westward Ho!, named after the novel by Charles Kingsley, is the only place name in the United Kingdom that officially contains an exclamation mark. There is a town in Quebec called Saint-Louis-du-Ha! Ha!, which is spelled with two exclamation marks. The city of Hamilton, Ohio, changed its name to Hamilton! in 1986. The city of Ostrava, Czech Republic, even changed its logotype to Ostrava!!! in 2008.

Exlibris A bookplate, also known as ex-librs (Latin: "from the books of ..."), is usually a small print or decorative label pasted into a book, often on the inside front cover, to indicate its owner. Simple typographical bookplates are termed "book labels".

Experimental Jetset's iconic "Helvetica List" Shirt.

Experimental Jetset is an Amsterdam design studio who were the first ones to use the meanwhile well-known "Helvetica List" style. Their John & Paul & Ringo & George shirt from 2001 became an iconic and many times copied piece of streetwear. The fact that they used an ampersand ("&") after each name had a purely formal reason. This way, the list of names looked more even.

Expert font An additional font designed to accompany a standard font, providing a range of characters like small capitals, ligatures, old-style figures, etc.

$bold$

Extenders.

Extenders The part of a letter which extends above the mid line, such as "b" or "d".

Eye The right eye perceives colours differently than the left. Reason: The optical signals of the right eye are processed in the left brain where the Language Centre operates. By unconscious language associations greenish blues and bluish greens are distinguished much more quickly in the left margin of our visual field than in the right.

F

Facsimile A reproduction of an old book, manuscript, map, art print or other item that is as true to the original source as possible.

Fagen, Donald American singer (Steely Dan) who confessed in the song "New Frontier" on his solo CD The Nightfly that he desired to study design: "Well, I can't wait till I move to the city / Till I finally make up my mind / To learn design and study overseas".

Fairey, Shepard is an American contemporary street artist, illustrator and activist who became widely known for his Barack Obama "Hope" poster in 2008. He is also the founder of OBEY Clothing who emerged from the skateboarding scene.

False Friend False friends are words in two languages (or letters in two alphabets) that look or sound similar, but differ significantly in meaning. An example is the English embarrassed and the Spanish embarazada (which means pregnant).

Family of Man, the is the most successful photography post-war exhibition of all time. First installed in 1955 at the Museum of Modern Art, New York, it went on to tour the world and has been visited by more than 10 million people. The exhibition was curated by Edward Steichen, the director of the MOMA's Department of Photography. After two world wars it was his aim to promote world peace and equality. He collected 503 photographs, taken by 273 different (often unknown) photographers, and grouped them by theme. "The exhibition was meant to be understood around the world without the need for words" says Anke Reitz, conservator of The Family of Man in Luxembourg, where the collection has been installed since 1994.

ABCDEFGHIJKLM NOPQRSTUVWXYZ

Example of a Fat Face Type:
Gravitas One. Design: Sorkin Type.

Fat Faces are very heavy advertising typefaces that are related to Didone types but much bolder. Around 1803 Robert Thorne, who was also responsible for coining the term Egyptian to describe what is generally known today as the Slab Serif, designed the first Fat Face.

Faux bold is a typeface that is set to bold even though a true bold version does not exist in the standard set.

Features of Letters

No Arcs . . . AEFHIKLMNTVWXYZ
No straight lines . . . . COS
Sym (horiz) . . . . BCDEHIKOX
Sym (vert) . . . . AHIMOTUVWXY
Roman numerals . . . . CDILMVX
Morse code (Points only) . . . . . EHIS
Morse code (Strokes only) . . . . MOT
Same look on head . . . . . . HINOSXZ

Federalist flag, the The federalist flag, also known as the Flag of the European Movement, is a flag commonly used up to the adoption of the European flag with the ring of twelve stars. It is speculated that the man most likely to have proposed it was Duncan Sandys, British Conservative and the son-in-law of Winston Churchill.

FedEx The FedEx logo was created in 1994 by Lindon Leader. FedEx is a syllabic abbreviation of the company's original name: Federal Express. At first glance the logo seems pretty simple until the detail discovered: a right-pointing arrow located in the negative space between the "E" and "X", which stands for forward movement and thinking.

FedEx logo, 1994. Design: Lindon Leader.

Fehlbaum, Rolf is well-known as the Chairman Emeritus and active Member of the Board of Directors of Vitra, a family-owned furniture company. Only a few people know that he completed his academic studies in 1967 with a doctoral thesis, written under the supervision of Edgar Salin, on the topic of Saint-Simonism.

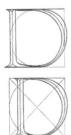

Feliciano's design for the letter D from his Alphabetum Romanum, 1463.

Feliciano, Felice was an Italian calligrapher living in the 15th century. He was the first to geometrically recreate the Roman inscriptions.

Fella, Ed American graphic designer, artist and AIGA Medalist Ed Fella was a late starter. He received his Master of Fine Arts in design at Cranbrook Academy of Art, at age 47.

The Federalist flag consists of a large green "E" upon a white field.

Fetter, William was an American graphic designer who was the first to create a human figure as a 3D model, called "The First Man". The First Man was a pilot in a short computer animation from 1964. Fetter also helped to coin the term "Computer graphics".

Finial.

Finial A finial is a curved end.
Fischer, Volker The Curator of Design at the Frankfurt Museum of Applied Art used to rhyme in his opening speeches. For the exhibition "Ornament and Promise", for instance, was opened by Fischer with the rhyme: "Character's a surface matter, asceticism e'er spoils the latter."

Fisher Price

Fisher Price released a movable type Printer's Kit, designed for children, in 1981.

Francis Hopkinson's flag for the US, featuring 13 six-pointed stars arranged in rows.

Flag of the United States The current design of the US flag is its 27th. Designer of the first stars and stripes flag was Francis Hopkinson of New Jersey, a naval flag designer in 1777. Since then the flag design constantly changed because more states became parte of the US. Today, the 50 stars on the flag represent the 50 states of the United States of America, and the 13 stripes represent the thirteen British colonies that declared independence from the Kingdom of Great Britain.

Fleckhaus, Willy was a German graphic designer best known for his colourful corporate design for the publisher Suhrkamp. Less known is that he comissioned Max Bill to design his house in Bergisches Land. Oswald Mathias Unger was the responsible architect.

Flexography A technique where printing plates are made of rubber or soft plastic material and then stretched around a drum on the press that rotates.

Flusser, Villém In his youth the later design theorist sought a personal meeting with author Franz Kafka, who, like Flusser, was born in Prague.

Focal Point The focal point is where you want to draw the reader's or viewer's eye.

Font A complete combination of characters created in a specific type, style, and size. The set of characters in a font entails the letter set, the number set, and all of the special characters and marks you get when pressing the shift key or other command keys on your keyboard.

Form follows function Form follows function is a principle associated with modernist architecture and industrial design in the 20th century. The principle is that the shape of a building or object should be primarily based upon its intended function or purpose. In 1896 American architect Louis H. Sullivan wrote an essay with the title: "The tall office building artistically considered." There it says: "Whether it be the sweeping eagle in his flight, or the open apple-blossom, the toiling workhorse, the blithe swan, the branching oak, the winding stream at its base, the drifting clouds, over all the coursing sun, form ever follows function, and this is the law."

Forty 40, "forty" is the only number in which the letters are in alphabetical order.

Four-colour process, the is a printing technique that creates colours by combining, cyan, magenta, yellow, and black.

Fornasetti, Piero was an Italian painter and interior designer, who created more than 11,000 items such as scarves, ties, lamps, furni-

ture, china plates and tables. Many featuring the face of a woman, operatic soprano Lina Cavalieri, as a motif. Fornasetti found her face in a 19th-century magazine.

Fournier's type construction, 1737.

Fournier, Pierre-Simon was a mid-18th century punch-cutter, type-founder. His main accomplishment is that he "created a standardized measuring system that would revolutionize the typography industry forever". This system was further developed by François Didot into the point based system that still exists today.

Fraktur The 1941 Nazi decree that banned the use of Fraktur was printed on letterhead set in Fraktur type. Isn't that ironic? They probably didn't know the typographic details.

Frankfurt Kitchen As part of the New Frankfurt-project Margarete Schütte-Lihotzky created the famous Frankfurt Kitchen in 1926, which was the prototype of the built-in kitchen now prevalent in the western world. Based on the scientific research by US management expert Frederick Winslow Taylor and her own research, Li-

hotzky used a railroad dining car kitchen as her model to design a "housewife's laboratory" using a minimum of space and time but offering a maximum of comfort and equipment to the working mother. Schütte-Lihotzky calculated the distances that would be traversed while working in it with the aid of a stop-watch, so as to locate the frequently-used elements.

"Skyscraper" Step Table, late 1920s. Design: Paul T. Frankl. © Brooklyn Museum.

Frankl, Paul Theodore was an Austrian Art Deco furniture designer and architect who became famous for his celebrated skyscraper style, a symbol of American modernity in the 1920s.

Franklin Gothic is a sans-serif type designed by Morris Fuller Benton (1872–1948) in 1902 that has become very popular in many advertisements and headlines, especially in newspapers. It was named in honour of Benjamin Franklin who was a leading author, printer, and one of the Founding Fathers of the United States.

MoMA

Logo of the Museum of Modern Art New York, set in Franklin Gothic.

Fregio Megano is a modular font of Italian origin created in the 1920s composed of 20 different elements. The designer is unknown.

ABCDEFGHI

Fregio Megano typeface.

Frigidaire Raymond Loewy's Refrigerator "Frigidaire" from 1955 was deliberately crafted to remind one of a Cadillac once the fridge door being slammed.

Frequency modulation The term frequency modulation is used to refer to a halftone print technique. Where continuous tone imagery contains an infinite range of colours or greys, the halftone process reduces visual reproductions to an image that is printed with only one colour of ink, in dots of differing spacing.

Fridolin. © Frog Design.

Fridolin was the Nickname of the frog that became the heraldic beast of frog design. The frog did really work for frog design as a weather forecaster.

Frisch, Max The swiss author completed his diploma in architecture in 1942. That same year he created the spaciously laid out outdoor swimming pool Letzigraben in Zurich, which is still in use today.

Frankfurt Kitchen, 1926.

Frontispiece A book frontispiece refers to a decorative or informative illustration facing a book's title page. While some books depict thematic elements, other books feature the author's portrait as the frontispiece. The word derives from the French word "frontispiece", meaning Front side and from the latin "frontispicium", "frons" means forehead and "spicere" means to see.

Fukuda, Shigeo was a Japanese sculptor, graphic artist and poster designer who was famous for his optical illusions. One of his best-known works, called "Victory 1945", features a projectile heading straight at the opening of the barrel of a cannon.

Fuller, Richard Buckminster was an American architect, systems theorist, author, designer, and inventor. Fuller published more than 30 books, coining or popularizing terms such as "Spaceship Earth", ephemeralization, and synergetic. He also developed numerous inventions, mainly architectural designs. An allotrope of carbon, fullerene – and a specific molecule of that allotrope C60 (buckminsterfullerene or buckyball) has been named after him for their structural and mathematical resemblance to geodesic spheres.

turist movement. The first Futurist Manifesto was written and published in 1909. The subject was a rejection of past and a celebration of speed, machinery and industry.

The commemorative plaque left on the Moon in July 1969 features text set in Futura.

Futhark runes on "The Kylver stone".

Futhark is a phonetic alphabet consisting of runes. The name is derived from the first six letters: f, u, th, a, r, k;

Futura Designed by Paul Renner in 1927, Futura was the prototype of a geometric sans-serif Linear-Antiqua.

Futurist Manifesto Filippo Marinetti was an Italian poet, editor, art theorist, and founder of the Fu-

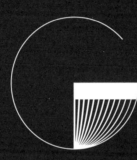

Games, Abram was one of the most important graphic designers of 20th century. He designed some of Britain's most iconic images including the "Join the ATS" recruitment poster of 1941, also known as "The Blonde Bombshell". Besides his bold graphic posters, he also pioneered in designing the first moving on-screen symbol of BBC Television in 1954.

Old and new Gap logo.

Gap In 2010, the clothing company introduced a new logo that only lasted for a week.

Garamond, Claude was a French publisher and one of the leading type designers. He was also one of the first independent punchcutters and is recognised for the elegance of his typefaces. Less known is that many "Garamond" revivals are actually based on the work of Jean Jannon, whose work was for some years misattributed to Garamond.

Garfunkel, Art The famous musician lists every book he read since June 1968 on his homepage.

Garland, Ken is a British graphic designer, photographer, writer and educator. His most famous piece of writing about the ethics of graphic design is the First Things First manifesto of 1964. Here is an excerpt of it: "... we have reached a saturation point at which the high pitched scream of consumer selling is no more than sheer noise. We think that there are other things

more worth using our skill and experience on. There are signs for streets and buildings, books and periodicals, catalogues, instructional manuals, industrial photography, educational aids, films, television features, scientific and industrial publications and all the other media through which we promote our trade, our education, our culture and our greater awareness of the world ..." – Ken Garland, First Things First, 1964.

"Join the ATS poster", 1941. Design: Abram Games.

Garrett, Malcolm is a well-known British graphic designer whose London studio was the first to go totally digital in 1990. Besides that he is known for his iconic record covers for music artists such as Duran Duran, Buzzcocks, Simple Minds, and Peter Gabriel.

Lou Dorfsman in front of the typographic wall, 1966. © www.typx-blog.com.

Gatefold A type of fold in which the paper is folded inward to form four or more panels.

Gastrotypographicalassemblage is a 35 feet wide by 8.5 feet tall work of typographic art designed by Lou Dorfsman to decorate the cafeteria in Eero Saarinen's CBS Building in New York City. The wall is made out of hand-milled wood type. The project was completed in 1966 with assistance from graphic designer Herb Lubalin, and Tom Carnase.

Gaul, Albro T. Gaul's book "The Wonderful World of Insects" designed in 1953 by Stefan Salter was the first book made with phototypesetting.

Gautschen The so-called German term "Gautschen" is an old book printer custom from the 16th century, in which an apprentice after passing the final examination, is submerged in a tub and/or set on a wet sponge. In its original meaning, the term "Gautschen" refers to the first dewatering step after scooping the paper and the deposition of freshly made paper sheet from the screen onto a felt pad.

Gehry, Frank is not only one of the most important architects of the 20th century, he also designed furniture, clothing, jewellery and sculptures. His first line of furniture, produced from 1969 to 1973, was called "Easy Edges", made out of cardboard.

Gentleman's Magazine, the was founded and first published by Edward Cave in 1731 in London. It is considered to be the first to use the term magazine (from the French magazine, meaning "Storehouse".) It was released monthly and reported of news and commentary on any topic the educated public might be interested in.

Georgia is a typeface designed in 1993 by Matthew Carter, named after a tabloid headline which reads "Alien heads found in Georgia."

German Dictionary, the is the largest and most comprehensive dictionary of the German language in existence. Less known is that the German Dictionary was authored by the Brothers Grimm, known for their fairy tales, in 1838.

Gerstner, Karl is a popular Swiss graphic designer and typographer. Less known is that he also wrote and designed a cookbook with good health in mind, named Avantgarde Cuisine, Publisher Arthur Niggli, 1990.

Gesamtkunstwerk is a German word which has been accepted in English as a term in aesthetics. It is translated as total work of art or universal artwork that makes use of all or many art forms. The term was first used by the German writer and philosopher K. F. E. Trahndorff in an essay in 1827.

Gibson, William created the term "Cyberspace" in 1984 in his novel "Neuromancer".

Girard, Alexander was a product and textile designer, who is best known for his fabrics created for the designs of George Nelson and Charles and Ray Eames. Less known is that in 1962, Girard and his wife established the Girard Foundation in Santa Fe to manage their art collection that numbered over 100,000 pieces, including toys, dolls and other ethnic expressions.

Giugiaro, Giorgetto is an Italian automobile designer, widely recognised as one of the finest and most prolific car designers. He also developed a new pasta shape, called "Marille". Its shape was inspired by the automobile door gasket section.

Giugiaro's pasta "Marille". © Photo & Multimedia Archives Italdesign-Giugiaro S.p.A.

Ghosting The appearance of a faint image coming on a printed sheet because of ink starvation.

GIF short for Graphics Interchange Format supports animation and allows an individual palette of 256 colour for each frame.

Ginzburg, Ralph was an American author, publisher and photo-journalist. In 1962, Ginzburg began to publish his first major work, Eros. A periodical magazine containing articles on love and sex which was art directed by Herb Lubalin. Only four issues of Eros were published, because Ginzburg was indicted under federal obscenity laws for sending obscene material through US mail.

Gismondi, Ernesto The founder of the Italian business Artemide uses the pseudonym Örni Halloween, when designing lamps for his own company.

The "I Love New York" logo, 1977. Design: Milton Glaser.

Glaser, Milton Glaser's original sketch to accompany the agency's "I Love New York" slogan was conceived in a taxi over to a meeting for the campaign. It comprised the letter I and a heart shape followed by NY, all on the same line. As the idea developed he decided to stack the I and heart shape on a line above the NY characters.

Global Tools was an Italian Initiative to support alternative ideas and experiences on design and art. The Global Tools movement was founded in 1973 by well-known designers and architects, including Ettore Sottsass Jr. and Alessandro Mendini, members of the groups Archizoom and Superstudio and many more. The initiative only lasted 2 years but had a great influence on later groups like Studio Alchimia or Memphis Design.

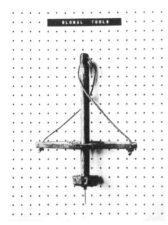

Global Tools Bulletin, 1973. © Global Tools.

Gloor, Beat is a writer and lecturer and well-known for his book "Staatsexamen". He also invented a slot machine that mixes up random syllables to form new words and meanings: www.be-deuts.ch.

Glyph In typography, a glyph is any graphic symbol: letter, number, punctuation mark, space, etc. A font is actually a collection of glyphs. The word is derived from the Greek word for "carving".

Goertz, Albrecht von was a German industrial designer who designed cars for BMW including the BMW 503 and BMW 507, which is widely considered one of the most elegant sportscars ever.

Goethe, Johann W. von Goethe's "Faust 1" became the first paperback in 1867.

Goldfish The goldfish can perceive the widest range of colours of all living beings.

BMW 507. Design: Goertz von Albrecht. Photo Credits: Michael Furman. © 2013 Courtesy of RM Auctions.

Gomringer, Eugen is often called the father of concrete poetry. Only a few people know that he also worked as a secretary for Max Bill at the famous Ulm School of Design from 1954 to 1957.

Good Design The "Good Design" movement was a design concept that started in the 1930s in the United States and included names like Charles and Ray Eames, László Moholy-Nagy and Hans Wegner. Today, "Good Design" is a federally protected trademark of the Chicago Athenaeum Museum of Architecture and Design.

Google In 2000, the search engine Google started hiring Illustrators from all over the world to create logos for special events. These special logos have become known as Google Doodles.

Gotham is a family of geometric sans-serif digital typefaces created by American type designer Tobias Frere-Jones in 2000. Gotham has been highly visible in Barack Obama's 2008 presidential campaign as well as on the cornerstone of the One World Trade Center.

Graham, John J. was an American graphic artist who designed and created the first NBC peacock logo in 1956.

ABCDEFGHIJKLMNO
PQRSTUVWXYZÀÅÉ
ÎÕØÜabcdefghijklmn
opqrstuvwxyzàåéîõø
&1234567890($£.,!?)

Gotham font, 2000. Design: Tobias Frere-Jones.

Graphem A unit of a writing system consisting of all the written symbols or sequences of written symbols that are used to represent a single phoneme.

9093 Kettle, 1985. Design: Michael Graves. © Alessi.

Graves, Michael was a recognized American architect and member of the Italian Memphis Group. Besides his famous architectural buildings he is probably best known for having designed a stainless steel teakettle featuring a red whistle in the shape of a bird for Alessi in 1985. The so called 9093 Teakettle became the company's all-time bestselling product.

Gray, Eileen was an Irish furniture designer and architect and a pioneer of the Modern Movement in architecture. Gray opened up a small shop in Paris, which she ran from 1922 until 1930. She chose the male pseudonym "Jean Desert" for her gallery, because she believed that a male name would be more acceptable to her clientele.

Greiman, April is recognized as one of the first designers to embrace computer technology as a design tool and became a visionary pioneer of digital design. Best known is her iconic video image "Does it Make Sense?" for Design Quarterly #133, composed and reproduced using a Mac Plus computer.

Greeking is the use of nonsense or dummy text, instead of the real body copy. The aim is not to distract from the design layout. The nonsense text is often Latin, for example the well-known "Lorem ipsum". Greeking also refers to Page layout tools, such as QuarkXpress, which greys out the text to speed up the display of a layout on screen.

Griffo, Francesco was a Venetian punchcutter in 15th century, who worked for Aldus Manutius, founder of Aldine Press. Griffo developed the first *italic* as a handwritten style. It was designed to conserve space on a page so that the books Manutius published could take a smaller form.

Grillo The first folding Telephone named "Grillo" was developed by Richard Sapper and Marco Zanuso in 1965. The device that at first reminds one of a PC mouse integrates listing, speaking and dialing

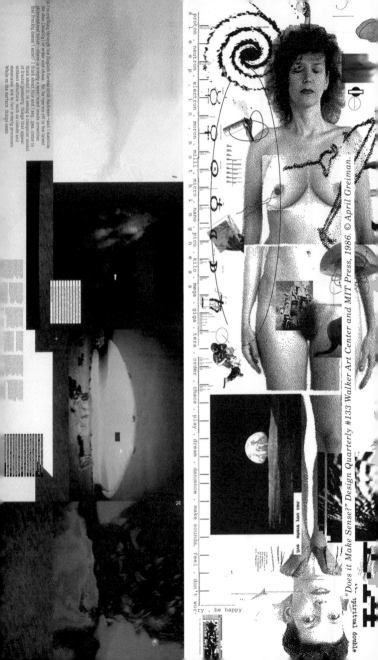

"Does it Make Sense?" Design Quarterly #133 Walker Art Center and MIT Press, 1986. © April Greiman.

functions. The moment one picks up the apparatus, the telephone's microphone, unfolds.

Grillo Telephone, 1965. Design: Richard Sapper and Marco Zanuso for Siemens Italtel. © Richard Sapper.

Gropius, Walter was a German architect and founder of the Bauhaus School, who, together with Ludwig Mies van der Rohe, Le Corbusier and Frank Lloyd Wright, is widely regarded as one of the pioneering masters of modern architecture. Less known is that he wrote a letter to his mother about his lack of drawing skills. He wrote: "My total lack of ability to commit to paper even the most simple object, spoils many beautiful thing for me and makes me view with apprehension my future profession."

Groundwood are low cost papers, such as newsprint.

Guardian, the is a British national daily newspaper founded in 1821. It is still referred to by its nickname of "The Grauniad" because of its regularly made typographical errors.

Guerrilla marketing often uses unconventional forms of communication, in unexpected places, and focuses on low-cost strategies that create a high-impact impression. The term was first coined by Jay Conrad Levinson in 1984.

Gugelot Design was once Europe's largest design corporation based in Böfingen, near Ulm. They had to close in 1974, among other things because the Swedish Beckmann Cars AB was not able to pay for the bright-red "fully plastic safety sportscar" it had commissioned, which never went into series production.

GUI short for graphical user interface, that allows users to interact with all kinds of electronic devices through graphical icons, instead of typed command labels or text navigation.

Guillemets also known as angle quotes or French quotation marks, are polylines pointed like arrows. They appear either double « hi » or single ‹ hi › and shouldn't be mistaken for the "less than" (<) and "greater than" (>) symbols. The word Guillemet derives from Guillaume Le Bé, a French printer and punchcutter.

Guixé, Martí is a Spanish designer living in Barcelona and Berlin. He filled a roll-on deodorant holder with Prussian blue ink and thus created a giant ballpoint pen.

Gutter The white space formed by the inner margins of a spread near the books spine.

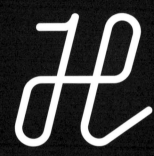

Häberli, Alfredo is a Swiss product designer who worked for companies like Zanotta or Iittala. In 2003 he advertised Windsor Clothing alongside Danish super-model Helena Christensen. The idea to feature Häberli came from design studio Achermann.

Haeckel, Ernst was not only a zoologist but also an accomplished artist and illustrator, who inspired a lot of product designers, especially the Art Nouveau Movement with his colourful "Art forms of Nature" of 1904.

Haiku is a very short form of Japanese poetry which consists of 17 syllables in three phrases of 5, 7, and 5 on respectively. In Japanese, haiku are traditionally printed in a single vertical line while haiku in English often appear in three lines to parallel the three phrases of Japanese haiku.

Hairline The thin strokes of a serif typeface or the thinnest possible line that can be reproduced.

Half title The title of a book printed at the top of the first page of the text or on a full page preceding the main title page. The half title is usually counted as the very first page in a printed book.

Halftone is the reprographic technique that simulates continuous tone imagery through the use of dots, varying either in size or in spacing, thus generating a gradient like effect. "Halftone" can also be used to refer specifically to the image that is produced by this process.

Halloween, Örni Under this pseudonym Ernesto Gismondi designs lighting for its Italian company Artemide in 1958.

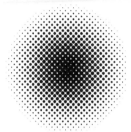

Halftone Circle.

Hamilton, Richard From the mid-1960s, the British artist Richard Hamilton was represented by art dealer Robert Fraser, who recommended Hamilton's work to Paul McCartney. They became friends resulting in him producing the cover design and poster collage for the Beatles' White Album. The white surface bearing the blind-embossed name of the band and with a serial number printed on it was a reaction by Hamilton to the work of his colleague Peter Blake, who had devised the jam-packed cover of the precursor album Sgt. Pepper.

Han characters are ideographic characters used in the writing of Chinese and some other Asian languages.

Harrison, Christopher Guy is a British luxury furniture designer, who patented one of his designs: the iconic Chris-X (pronounced kris-krôs) leg design. The chair was inspired by "The corseted waist-line of Scarlett O'hara in Gone with the Wind and the crossed legs of a ballerina", Harrison explained.

Hawaii The Hawaiian alphabet has only 12 letters: a, e, i, o, u, p, k, m, n, w, l and h.

*Boudoir chair with Chis-X legs, 1960.
Design: Christopher Guy Harrison.*

Heartfield, John was a German
artist and designer who designed
book jackets and stage sets for
Bertolt Brecht and Erwin Pisca-
tor. Heartfield, formerly known as
Helmut Herzfeld, was the first to
produce photomontages, especially
political ones during the 1930s
and 1940s.

*Heartfield's "The Hand has 5 Fingers",
1928. Attribution: Bundesarchiv, 102-
05929 / CC-BY-SA 3.0.*

Heizölrückstoßabdämpfung is the
longest German isogram (no letter
repeats) that makes any sense. See
page 84 to know what it means.

Helvetica is one of the most popular typefaces of the 20th century.
Originally named Neue Haas Grotesk (New Haas Grotesque), it was
rapidly licensed by Linotype and
renamed Helvetica, being similar
to the Latin adjective for Switzerland, Helvetia.

Helvetica Bold Typeface.

Henrion, Frederick Henri Kay was
a German graphic designer, known
first for his wartime posters and
exhibitions for the Ministry of Information during the War, he later
became one of the founding fathers
of modern corporate identity. His
clients included: British European
Airways, KLM London Electricity
Board and The National Theatre,
just to name a few.

*KLM logo, 1961. Design: F.H.K. Hen-
rion.*

Hergé Georges Prosper Remi alias Hergé was a Belgian cartoonist. He is best known for creating "The Adventures of Tintin", the series of comic albums which are considered one of the most popular European comics of the 20th century. Less known is that he again and again referred to contemporary design in his "Adventures of Tintin". In the episode "Tintin in Tibet" Professor Calculus sits on a chair entitled "Visiteur", which Jean Prouvé designed in 1941.

Métropole Visiteur FV 12 armchair, 1948. © Ateliers Jean Prouvé.

Hexachrome A six-colour printing process designed by Pantone Inc., that uses six primary colours (cyan, magenta, yellow, orange, green, and black) to simulate a full range of colours. The hexachrome process was discontinued by Pantone in 2008.

Hickey A spot in printing caused by dirt or hardened specks of ink. A hickey is also called a bulls eye or a fish eye.

Highway Gothic is a set of sans-serif typefaces developed by the United States Federal Highway Administration. It was released in 1948 and is used for road signage in the US, Canada, Turkey, Mexico, Australia, Norway, Spain, Venezuela, the Netherlands, Brazil, Chile, China, Taiwan, Malaysia, Indonesia, India, Mongolia, Ecuador and New Zealand, and some signs in Saudi Arabia, when written in English. Based on Highway Gothic, Tobias Frere-Jones designed Interstate.

Hilton, James is an English designer who co-founded the creative agency AKQA and the product design company AtelierStrange. As a pioneer in design and creativity, Hilton has collected several global awards and is also an executive member of The International Academy of Digital Arts and Sciences. IADAS is an international organization founded in 1998 whose members include David Bowie, Francis Ford Coppola and Richard Branson, just to name a few.

United States Federal Highway Sign.

Hipgnosis was an English art design group based in London that specialised in creating record covers for notable rock bands, including Pink Floyd, Led Zeppelin, AC/DC, Def Leppard, Genesis, Peter Gabriel, The Police and many more. Their style is best described as "hypnotic" and "futuristic" at the same time. Hipgnosis achieved international fame with their iconic cover design for Pink Floyd's The Dark Side of the Moon in 1973.

Music-cupboard Braun HM 6-81. Design: Herbert Hirche. © Christos Vittoratos.

Hirche, Herbert was a German architect and furniture- and product designer. Hirche studied from 1930 to 1933 at the Bauhaus in Dessau and Berlin. From 1934 to 1938 he worked in Mies van der Rohe's office in Berlin, until his boss emigrated to the United States. Music cabinets by Braun, designed by Herbert Hirche were found in the late 1950s in every modern villa in central Europe, many architects recommended these devices to equip their buildings.

HKS is an abbreviation of three German manufacturers of colours: Hostmann-Steinberg Druckfarben, Kast + Ehinger Druckfarben, and H. Schmincke & Co. The HKS colour system contains 120 spot colours and 3520 tones for coated and uncoated paper.

Hobo Signs Beginning in the early 1880s, during their travels for work, hoboes, also known as migratory workers or homeless vagabonds, made marks with chalk, paint or coal on walls, sidewalks, fences and posts. The signs were meant to let others know what was ahead.

Hobo Signs for Safe Camp: "Camp here and Someone Home".

Hoffmann, Josef was an Austrian architect and designer of consumer goods. The iconic Sitzmaschine, the "machine for sitting", was originally designed by him for his Purkersdorf Sanatorium in Vienna. It represents one of Hoffmann's earliest experiments in unifying a building and its furnishings as a total work of art.

Sitzmaschine, 1905. Design: Josef Hoffmann.

Hope The Barack Obama "Hope" poster is an image of Barack Obama designed by street artist and illustrator Shepard Fairey. The photograph which was uncredited used by Fairey as the basis of the iconic Hope poster was actually taken by Mannie Garcia, an American freelance photojournalist, in April 2006. The original poster design was created in a single day, and quickly went viral. As Obama's campaign progressed parody posters featuring opponents Sarah Palin and John McCain appeared.

Horgan, Stephen H. is credited with the first printed photo using a halftone screen, which was released in the "New York Daily Graphic" on December 2, 1873. The photo showed an image of Steinway Hall in Manhattan.

Horntrich, Günter The founder of Yellow Design and Professor of Ecology and Design at KISD was German Vice Champion in pair skating in the 60s.

Hot Spot Printing defect caused when a piece of dirt or an air bubble caused incomplete draw-down during contact platemaking, leaving an area of weak ink coverage.

House Sheet Paper kept in stock by a printer and suitable for a variety of printing jobs. Also called floor sheet.

How High the Moon is the name of a chair, designed by Shiro Kuramata in 1986, who is one of Japan's most important designers of the 20th century. The chair, named after a jazz title of Duke Ellington, is completely made of wire steel mesh and became one of the most desirable design objects. The "How High the Moon" two seater was sold for $24,000.00 at Bonhams London in 1998.

HTML Abbreviation for HyperText Markup Language. HTML is used as the source language for a web page.

HTTP Abbreviation for HyperText Transfer Protocol. It manages the communications between servers and clients.

DreamWorks Logo, 1995. Design: Robert Hunt, featuring his own son.

Hunt, Robert is an American illustrator who was commissioned by Stephen Spielberg to create the DreamWorks logo in 1995. The boy, fishing from the moon, featured in the logo is Hunt's son Robert.

Huszár, Vilmos was a Hungarian painter and designer, who lived in the Netherlands. He co-founded the famous De Stijl magazine and designed the cover for the first issue.

Hypertext is text which contains links to other texts. The term was coined around 1965 by Ted Nelson, an American pioneer of information technology. He also coined the designation hypermedia, a nonlinear medium of information, including graphics, audio, video, plain text and hyperlinks.

Hyphen The hyphen (-) is a punctuation mark used to connect words and to separate syllables of a single word.

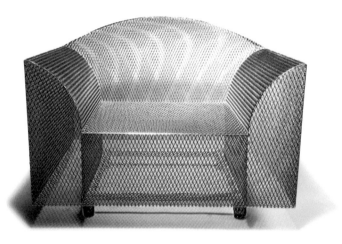

IBM

IX monogram

IBM International Business Machines, more commonly known as IBM, has created one of the world's most widely known brands. The trademark was developed by Paul Rand in 1972. It was designed from a geometrically constructed slab-serif typeface called City Medium, designed by Georg Tromp in 1930.

IBM logo, 1972. Design: Paul Rand.

Iceland In Iceland, all residents are using the alphabetical order of their first name in the phone book.

Ideograph A character or symbol representing an idea without expressing the punctuation of a specific word. Also known as Ideogram.

Igarashi, Takenobu is one of Japan's most prolific artists. He acclaimed international attention as a graphic designer in the mid-70s through his axonometric alphabets.

Ikarus is a type design and production software. It was developed by URW foundry to convert existing typefaces and logos into digital format.

IKEA The IKEA catalog is with 115 million copies, the highest printed object in the world. For the Asia edition of the IKEA catalog the living room facilities are arranged on only 10 m², since the apartments are smaller than in Europe. The products are labeled with men's names, fabrics with women's names and sofas with names of Swedish lakes.

Imposition Arrangement of pages on the printed sheet so they appear in the right sequence after folding.

Imprimatur Official approval or license to print or publish.

Incipit The opening words of a text at the beginning of some medieval manuscripts.

Incunable An incunable, or sometimes incunabulum, is a pamphlet, book, or broadside that was printed before the year 1501 in Europe. Incunable is the anglicised singular form of "incunabula", Latin for "swaddling clothes", which can refer to "the earliest stages or first traces in the development of anything." At this time it only existed 27,000 different incunables. A famous incunable is Johannes Gutenberg's B42-bible.

Example of a floral decorated Initial R.

Initial A letter at the beginning of the work, chapter, or paragraph that is sometimes decorated. The word is derived from the Latin initialis, which means standing at the beginning. Also referred to as dropcap.

Ink set-off Print sheets can rub off on each other when the colour is not completely dry or too much paint is on the sheet.

INK

Ink Traps on Bell Centennial.

Ink Trap is a feature of certain typefaces designed for printing in small sizes. At an ink trap, the corners or details are removed from the letterforms. When the type is printed, ink naturally spreads into the removed area. Without ink traps, the excess ink would soak outwards and ruin the crisp edge. Ink traps are only needed for small point sizes and are usually only found on typefaces designed for printing on newsprint. Typefaces featuring ink traps include Kurier, Bell Centennial.

Insertio 6.5 pt font size, especially for the set of advertisements.

Interleaves Printed pages loosely inserted in a publication.

International Symbol of Access, 1968. Design: Susanne Koefoed.

International Symbol of Access also known as the Wheelchair Symbol, was designed by Danish design student Susanne Koefoed in 1968. The symbol consists of a blue square overlaid in white with a stylized image of a wheelchair.

International Typeface Corporation, the was one of the world's first type foundries that had no history in the production of metal type. It was founded in New York in 1970 by Aaron Burns, Herb Lubalin, and Edward Rondthaler. Their most known typeface is probably ITC Avant Garde Gothic.

Interrobang The interrobang, also known as the interabang is a nonstandard punctuation mark. It combines combine the functions of the question mark and the exclamation mark. The glyph is a superimposition of these two marks: ?!

Interstate is a neo-grotesque sans serif typeface, designed by Tobias Frere-Jones between 1993–1999. The typeface is closely related to the FHWA Series fonts, a signage alphabet drawn for the US Federal Highway Administration in 1949.

Iribe, Paul was a French illustrator, and designer who was Coco Chanel's lover from 1931 to his death. It is believed that he was one of the first designers to use a personal trademark, in the form of a flower, called "La Rose d'Iribe" on his products.

ISO 7001 is a standard that specifies graphical symbols, like buffet or toilet icons for the purposes of public information. The latest version, ISO 7001 was published in December 2007. ISO means International Organization for Standardization.

Isogram An isogram (also known as a "non-pattern word") is a logological term for a word or phrase without a repeating letter. It is also used by some to mean a word or phrase in which each letter appears the same number of times, not necessarily just once. In the book Making the Alphabet Dance, Ross Eckler reports the word "subdermatoglyphic" as the longest English word (17 letters). The longest German isogram is "Heizölrückstoßabdämpfung" (heating oil recoil dampening) with 24 letters, closely followed by "Boxkampfjuryschützlinge" (box fight jury fosterlings) and "Zwölftonmusikbücherjagd"(twelve-tone music book chase) with 23 letters.

Isotype is a method of showing social, technological, biological and historical data in pictorial form. Isotype (International System of TYpographic Picture Education) was created by Otto Neurath, a Viennese philosopher, economist and social scientist. He stated that "visual education was always the prime motive behind Isotype."

Italic The style of letters that usually slope to the right. Used for emphasis within text.

Ito, Ora is a French designer who became famous for his fictional creations for big players like Apple, BIC or Gucci. He virtually created his own brand and then extended it into design commissions.

Itten, Johannes was a Swiss expressionist painter, designer, theorist and part of the core of the Bauhaus in Weimar. Itten is probably best known for his pioneering work with colour palettes and colour contrasts. Less known is that he was a follower of Mazdaznan, a fire cult originating in the United States. Itten's cult affinity created conflict with Walter Gropius which led to Itten's resignation from the Bauhaus.

The 12-hue colour circle, 1961.

IX monogram, the is an early Christian monogram formed by the combination of the letter "I" or Iota for IHSOYS (Jesus in Greek) and "X" or Chi for XPISTOS (Christ in Greek).

J The letter "J" originated as a swash letter "i", used for the letter "i" at the end of Roman numerals when following another "i".

John Lennon Desk, 1974. Design: Dakota Jackson.

Jackson, Dakota is an American furniture designer who started his career with a piece of furniture he designed for John Lennon. Lennon's wife Yoko Ono comissioned Jackson to build a desk with hidden compartments. The result was a small cubed-shaped table with secret pressure points that open the desk's compartments.

Arne Jacobsen cutlery set.
© Georg Jensen.

Jacobsen, Arne Jacobsen's furniture is not only found in living rooms all over the world, but also in Stanley Kubrick's 1968 masterpiece Space Odyssey 2001. They used Jacobsen's cutlery set "AJ" of 1957.

Jacket The protective paper cover of a hardbound book, also called the "dust cover".

Jandl, Ernst was an Austrian poet, writer and translator. He is known for his specially-humorous language arts of experimental poetry and typographic visualization. One of his famous creations is the poem "Ottos Mops". It tells the story about a master and his dog, which manages to only use one vowel, the "O".

First official Apple logo, designed by Rob Janoff in 1977. The colour stripes should reflect the fact that Macs had colour screens. © Apple Inc.

Janoff, Rob is an American graphic designer who is best known for his creation of the Apple logo. According to Steve Jobs, the company's name was inspired by his visit to an apple farm while on a fruitarian diet. Jobs thought the name "Apple" was "fun, spirited and not intimidating". Job's only direction to Janoff was "Don't make it cute".

Japanese email If Japanese want to express joy in an email, they don't write :-), but ^ - ^.

da eius libros nõ ipsius esse sed Dionysii & Z loniorû tradunt:qui iocãdi causa cõscribent ere idoneo dederunt.Fuerunt autẽ Menippi de lydis scripsit:Xanthûq; breuiauit.Secûdu tius stratonicus sophista.Quartus sculptor. xtus pictores:utrosq; memorat apollodorus. uolumina tredeci sunt.Neniæ:testamenta:e tæ ex deorum psona ad physicos & mathem: icosq;:& epicuri fœtus:& eas quæ ab ipsis rel ur imagines:& alia.

Roman typeface by Nicolas Jenson, from an edition of "Laertius", printed in Venice in 1475.

Jenson, Nicolas was a French type designer and printer. He was responsible for the development of the first full roman typeface, published in 1475. It was based on humanistic characteristics and was highly legible.

ABCDEFGHIJKLMNO PQRSTUVWXYZÀÅÉ ÎÕØabcdefghijklmno pqrstuvwxyzàåéîõø& 1234567890($£€.,!?)

ITC Johnston, 1999. Design: Richard Dawson and Dave Farey, based on a design from Edward Johnston.

Johnston, Edward was a British and Uruguayan craftsman. He is most famous for designing the sans-serif Johnston typeface that was used throughout the London Underground system until it was redesigned in the 1980s. Johnston also redesigned the famous roundel symbol used throughout the system.

Jones, Allen known for his work that feature female dolls also designed the famous Korova Milk Bar in Stanley Kubrick's cult film "Clockwork Orange".

Hella Jongerius buttons. © Jyri Engestrom.

Jongerius, Hella is a Dutch industrial designer who likes to mix tradition and contemporary. She has defined this design style, naming it "Dirty Realism".

Journeyman printer Historically, a printer who is a member of a guild. Guild members consisted of apprentices, journeymen and master printers.

Jordan, Paul was one of the three directors of AEG, the major German electrical appliances company. He was responsible for the appointment of Peter Behrens. He stated a sentence that can be considered as a kind of Credo of Comprehensive Design: "Don't you think that even an engineer, when he buys a motor, will take it apart to inspect it. Even as an expert he buys upon first impressions. An engine must look pretty much like a birthday present."

Joop, Wolfgang is a well-known German fashion designer. Less known is that in 1968, he wanted to become an art teacher. He studied at the College of Fine Arts and Design (HBK) in Brunswick in Northern Germany. There he attended the 101 course with Karl Duschek, who was the studio partner of Anton Stankowski.

JPEG short for Joint Photographic Electronic Group is a common process for compressing images.

The Pelican chair, 1939. Design: Finn Juhl. © www.interiori.com

Juhl, Finn was a Danish architect, product designer, who was one of the leading figures in the creation of "Danish design", although one of his iconic designs, the Pelican chair was described as a "tired walrus" and "aesthetics in the worst possible sense of the word".

Tibor Kalman

Günter Kupetz

Kalman, Tibor was an American graphic designer (1949–1999) of Hungarian origin. Kalman was well-known for his work as editor-in-chief of iconic Colours magazine. According to his wife Maira he named his daughter "Lulu Bodoni" and gave his son "Onomatopoeia" for a second name.

Kamekura, Yasuka was a Japanese graphic designer, famous for his colourfully minimalist poster designs. His work for the Tokyo 1964 Olympics marked the first time that photography was used to promote the event.

Kare, Susan is a graphic designer who created many of the interface elements for the Apple Macintosh in the 1980s.

Apple Macintosh icon set. © Apple Inc.

Kauffer, Edward McKnight may be best known for the posters that he produced for London Underground. The posters span many styles, including futurism, cubism, vorticism and even impressionist influences such as Japanese woodcuts.

Keeler, Christine The nude model is frequently, yet mistakely, associated with a chair designed by Arne Jacobsen. The famous picture by British photographer Lewis Morley propelled Arne Jacobsen's model 3107 chair to prominence. However, the actual chair used was an imitation, with a hand-hold aperture cut out of the back to avoid copyright infringement. The chair used is now in the Victoria and Albert Museum.

Christine Keeler 1963. Museum no. E.2-2002. © Victoria and Albert Museum, London / Lewis Morley.

Kepes, György was a Hungarian-born painter, photographer, designer, educator, and art theorist that had a huge impact on design and design education between 1930 and 1970. In 1942, Kepes had been asked by the US Army to offer advice on military and civilian urban camouflage.

Kern, the denotes a part of a type letter that overhangs the edge of the type block.

Kerning means the process of adjusting the spacing between pairs of characters that would, if set normally, be too far apart (such as the capitals letters A and V, for example). In a well-kerned font, the two-dimensional blank spaces between each pair of characters all have a visually similar area.

György Kepes, Photography: Robert Haiko, 1983. © Kepes Institut, Eger.

Key Plate The K in CMYK stands for key plate because in four-colour printing, cyan, magenta and yellow printing plates are carefully keyed, or aligned, with the key of the black key plate. Some sources suggest that the K in CMYK comes from the last letter in "black" and was chosen because B already means blue. Some sources claim this explanation, although useful as a mnemonic, is incorrect, that K comes only from "Key" because black is often used as outline and printed first.

𝔚ilhelm·𝔎lingſpor

Wilhelm Klingspor Gotisch, 1926. Design: Rudolf Koch.

Kicker A lead-in or short introduction found above the headline. Usually set in a smaller or different type than the headline.

Kiesler, Frederick John was an Austrian-American theatre and product designer, whose objects were inspired by early biomorphism, using shapes reminiscent of nature and living organisms.

Kiss Impression Lightest possible impression that will transfer ink to a Substrate.

The "Le Klint 101" or "the Fruit Lantern", 1944. Design: Kaare Klint. © Le Klint A/S.

Klint, Kaare was a Danish architect and furniture designer, known as the father of modern Danish furniture design. His lamp "The Le Klint 101" or "the Fruit Lantern", originally made out of paper was created in 1944 and is still one of his bestsellers.

Koch, Rudolf was a German type designer. He is especially known for his blackletter typefaces, such as Kochschrift and Wilhelm Klingspor Gotisch, that were greatly influenced by hand-written manuscripts and Gothic letterforms.

Kraft Paper Strong paper used for wrapping and to make grocery bags and large envelopes.

Kramer, Ferdinand

Kramer, Ferdinand is not only famous for his architectural work, he also patented a vulcanite fender, while in the US in the 1940s. Unfortunately the vulcanite fender never found their way to mass-production.

Futura Bold Oblique

Example of Barbara Kruger's work, set in Futura Bold Oblique.

Kruger, Barbara is an American designer and conceptual artist who started her career as a magazine designer and art director for Condé Nast. Today her artworks feature topics like consumerism, feminism and classicism, in white-on-red Futura Bold Oblique or Helvetica Ultra Condensed overlaid on black and white photographs.

Heinrich Kühn's "Stillleben2", 1908.

Kühn, Heinrich was an Austrian-German photographer, who is regarded one of the forefathers of fine art photography and pioneer of using several innovative techniques, like Autochrome or his self-invented Syngraphie technique, that uses two negatives of different sensitivity to obtain a larger tonal spectrum.

"Karuselli", the most comfortable chair in the world, according to the New York Times, 1974.

Kukkapuro, Yrjö is a Finnish interior architect and furniture designer. His most famous design is called "Karuselli" and was nominated as the most comfortable chair in the world by The New York Times in 1974.

Kupetz, Günter His name perhaps doesn't sound familiar although he is one of the first famous designers of former German Federal Republic. Starting in the 1950s Kupetz created more than 1,000 products, including his iconic design for a mineral water bottle, also known as "Perlenflasche" (Pearl bottle) which was produced in a number of five billion pieces since 1971.

Lacoste The Lacoste logo heralds back to the days of René Lacoste who won the 1925 and 1928 Wimbledon tournaments. After a bet that he made with the Captain of the French Davis Cup team who promised him an expensive crocodile-skin suitcase, the American press nicknamed him "the Crocodile" and the brand was born.

Lacoste logo, 1923.

Lagerfeld, Karl Lagerfeld's father Otto Lagerfeld was besides being an inventor also the Manufacturer of the German Glücksklee-Brand of tinned Milk.

Channel 4 "Blocks" logo, 1982. Design: Martin Lambie-Nairn.

Lambie-Nairn, Martin is a British designer, filmmaker and director. He is acknowledged for having redefined television brand identity

design. Computer animation made it possible for him to produce what became regarded as a revolutionary identity for Channel 4, the "Blocks" logo, which was first published on 2nd November 1982.

Larsen, Jack Lenor is an American textile designer who worked for companies like Knoll, Pan Am and Braniff Airways. His unique hand-woven fabrics were also popular with clients such as Marilyn Monroe.

Peter László's console table designed as a tribute to Salvador Dalí.

László, Paul was a Hungarian architect and interior designer who had some famous admirers, including Salvador Dalí, Elizabeth Taylor or Barbara Streisand. However he was known for rejecting clients when he thought the relationship would be unsatisfactory to him.

Latin Alphabet, the also known as the Roman alphabet, is the most widely used script in the world today.

Lazarus, Emma was an American poet, born in New York City. She is best known for "The New Colossus", a sonnet written in 1883; its lines appear inscribed on a bronze plaque in the pedestal of the Statue of Liberty installed in 1903, a decade and a half after Lazarus's death.

Leading Refers to the amount of extra vertical space between lines of text.

Le Corbusier's signature.

Le Corbusier was a Swiss-French designer, painter and one of the pioneers of modern architecture. Le Corbusier, an altered form of his grandfather's name, "Lecorbésier", reflected his belief that anyone could reinvent themselves. Adopting a single name as a pseudonym was in vogue by artists during that era, especially in Paris.

Left: Stefan Lengyel, design for Monpti typewriter, 1968. Right: Ettore Sottsass, Valentine, 1969. © Monpti / Olivetti.

Lengyel, Stefan was assistant at the HfG Ulm design school in 1964, working with Hans Gugelot. The Hungarian designer created a type-writer for Monpti in 1968, a year before the lookalike of Sottsass went into production. Monpti was made in Czechoslovakia and marketed by German store Karstadt in 1971.

Lenna or Lena is one of the most widespread standard test image used in the field of image processing since 1973. It shows a photography of Lena Söderberg, shot by Dwight Hooker, cropped from the centrefold of Playboy magazine. The image gained its popularity largely because of an attractive woman appealed to the males in a male-dominated field.

BIC cigarette lighter, 1971. Design: Louis L. Lepoix. © BIC.

Lepoix, Louis L. The French engineer and designer came up with the design for the BIC Lighter in 1971. He today is almost forgotten, even though he has designed a wide range of products from lawn-mowers to airplanes.

Leporello The Leporello, a zigzag-sheet, takes its name from a character in the opera Don Giovanni: Leporello is the servant of Don Giovanni and maintains a list of the conquests of his master. Because the approximately 2,000 entries give a pretty long list, he folds the paper (probably by stairs) to make it more manageable.

Less is more The phrase "Less is more" is an Oxymoron. Architect Ludwig Mies van der Rohe adopted the motto „Less is more" to describe his aesthetic tactic of arranging the necessary components of a building to create an impression of extreme simplicity – he enlisted every element and detail to serve multiple visual and functional purposes; for example, designing a floor to also serve as the radiator, or a massive fireplace to also house the bathroom.

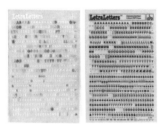

Letraset. © Neily Peelie.

Letraset is a company founded in London in 1959. Their original signature product was the Letraset Type Lettering System. This system consists of sheets of typefaces and other artwork elements that can be transferred to paper by dry rub-down.

Letter Gothic A monospaced typeface especially designed for the IBM Selectric typewriter by Roger Roberson in 1958. The engineer worked day and night on an alphabet whose characters were of a uniform width and all stood without bottom serifs on their imaginary baseline.

Letterpress A printing technique where movable type is inked and then pressed against paper. Also called block printing.

Letter Gothic

Letter Gothic, 1958.

Leupin, Herbert was a Swiss graphic designer known primarily for his poster work for Salem and Milka. Less known is that he also designed the logo for Art Basel, one of the most important international art fairs, in 1970.

Levi's 501 The brand name Levi's 501 was devised by the legendary American advertiser Mike Salisbury. In 1980 Salisbury converted this unspectacular set of digits into a worldwide known brand.

Ligature fj, ct and st.

Ligature Two or more letters are joined together to form one glyph. In addition to the functional ligatures fi, fl, ff, ffi, ffl, French typography has grammatical ligatures (Œ and œ) and, sometimes, the ornamental ligatures ct and st.

Link A stroke that connects the top and bottom bowls of lowercase double-story g's.

Linotype machine, the is a typesetting machine that could cast an entire line of type. It was invented by Ottmar Mergenthaler in 1890 and revolutionized typesetting, especially to set type for many pages on a daily basis. Before Mergenthaler's invention of the linotype in 1884, newspapers were limited to eight pages.

Link on the letter g.

Lipogram A lipogram (from Ancient Greek: leipográmmatos, "leaving out a letter") is a word game consisting of writing paragraphs or longer works in which a particular letter is avoided – usually a common vowel. Writing a lipogram may be a trivial task when avoiding uncommon letters like Z, J, Q, or X, but it is much more difficult to avoid common letters like E, T, or A, as the author must omit many ordinary words. A pangrammatic lipogram is a text that uses every letter of the alphabet except one. For example, "The quick brown fox jumped over the lazy dog" omits the letter S, which the usual pangram includes by using the word jumps.

Lissitzky, Lazar Markovich was a Russian artist, designer, photographer, typographer, polemicist and architect also known as El Lissitzky. He is one of the main figures of the Russian avantgarde, helping develop suprematism and influenced the Bauhaus and constructivist movements.

Loesch, Uwe is not only known for his iconic poster designs, he also wears one black and one white shoe on principle. His reason is simple: "Just for fun".

Pencil Sharpener, 1934. © Raymond Loewy.

Loewy, Raymond Loewy was one of the 20th century's most prolific and influential designers who also designed a teardrop pencil sharpener in 1934 that looks like it has been tested in a wind tunnel. It was one of Loewy's earlier designs that never went into production.

Coca-Cola's Typographic Logotype. © Coca-Cola.

Logo A logo is a graphic mark used by commercial enterprises, organizations and even individuals to promote instant public recognition. Logos can be symbols / icons, logotypes or wordmarks.

Longest English Sentence Jonathan Coe's The Rotters Club, published in 2001, contains a sentence with 13,955 words. It is currently the longest sentence in English Literature.

Longplayer is a computer generated piece of music that is designed to last for one thousand years. It started to play on 1 January 2000, and if all goes as planned, it will continue without repetition until 31 December 2999. It will restart on that date. The original music was composed by Jem Finer.

Egg

Loop on a double-story g.

Loop The enclosed or partially enclosed counter below the baseline of a double-story g.

Loos, Adolf The famous architect and influential European theorist of Modern architecture once received a letter by a satisfied customer which contained the lines: "Dear Mr. Loos. 30 years ago you furnished my home. I notice that my friends have their homes furnished anew every three years. Your furnishings are as good as new and still correspond with what I have in mind. Hence I am taking the liberty of enclosing your fee once again."

Lord Kitchener Wants You was a 1914 advertisement statement by Alfred Leete which became an army recruitment poster and one of the most iconic images of World War I. The poster depicted Lord Kitchener, the British Secretary of State for War, above the words "Wants You". This image has inspired numerous imitations, like Uncle Sam or John Bull.

Britain's Lord Kitchener Wants You Poster, 1914.

Lorem ipsum is a filler text used to demonstrate the graphic elements of a document without being distracted by the content. The Lorem ipsum text is derived from sections of Cicero's "De finibus bonorum et malorum", a 1st century BC Latin text.

Lorenz Static, the was designed by Richard Sapper in 1959 has frequently been the timer of choice for builders of bombs, because the mechanism of the clockwork originally used was taken from a torpedo guidance system.

The Lorenz Static, 1959. Design: Richard Sapper. © Richard Sapper.

Lovegrove, Ross is a Welsh industrial designer who started working for Frog Design in the early 80s for clients such as Sony and Apple. His main inspiration comes from organic forms and structures which became a new aesthetic expression for the 21st Century.

NSU Ro-80, 1967–77. Design: Claus Luthe. © **STAUD STUDIOS**

Lowercase The smaller form of letters in a typeface.

ABCDEFGHIJKLM
NOPQRSTUVWXYZ
abcdefghijklm
nopqrstuvwxyz
1234567890

Lucida Sans.

Lucida is a typeface superfamily made by Charles Bigelow and Kris Holmes in 1985. It was especially designed to be extremely legible when printed at small size or displayed on a low-resolution display. That's why it was so successfull on parts of Microsoft Windows and also as primary user interface font in Apple Inc.'s Mac OS X operating system until OS X Yosemite.

Lufthansa The Lufthansa corporate identity program became an international prototype for a consistent identity system with absolute uniformity. The program was designed by Otl Aicher in collaboration with Thomas Gonda, Fritz Querengasser and Nick Roericht in 1962.

Lufthansa logo, 1962.

Lustig, Alvin was a popular American book designer, graphic designer and typeface designer. Less known is that he was an accomplished magician as a teenager and a member of the International Brotherhood of Magicians.

Luthe, Claus was a German car designer, noted for his design work on the NSU Ro 80, Volkswagen K70 and numerous seminal models from Audi and BMW. He left his post at BMW after being accused of fatally stabbing his 33-year-old, chronically drug-dependent youngest son, Ulrich after an argument on Good Friday in 1990. He was eventually convicted of manslaughter and sentenced to

33 months in prison, but was released before having to serve the complete sentence.

Lutz, Rudolph was a product designer from the German Democratic Republic. In collaboration with Clauss Dietel he created products, which are among the classics of DDR designs, including the Heli-radio devices and the famous Wartburg 353.

Wartburg 353, 1965. © Ralf Christian Kunkel.

Lynch, David The famous film director even tried his hand at designing his own table. "I find most tables to be too large and too high; they eat into space and lead one to unpleasant thoughts", he explained.

Mackmurdo

M Weight

Mackmurdo, Arthur Heygate was an English architect and designer, who had a big influence on the Arts and Crafts Movement. Nikolaus Pevsner, a scholar of history of art, described Mackmurdo's use of foliage twisted into sinuous curves on the title page of the designer's own Wren's City Churches (1883) as "the first work of art nouveau which can be traced".

Madison Avenue is not only a street in Manhattan but was also a centre of American advertising in the 1960s.

Bookcover of Arthur Mackmurdo, Wren's City Churches, 1883.

Magazine 66% of all magazines, which are discarded along US highways, are pornographic.

Magenta is one of the four colours of ink used in colour printing and by an inkjet printer, along with cyan, yellow, and black. Magenta is named after a small Italian town, where the Battle of Magenta between France and Austria happened in 1859. To celebrate the victory, the French named the colour that had been invented that same year after the city. The web colour magenta is also called fuchsia.

Malevich, Kazimir was a Russian painter and art theoretician who became famous for his "Black square" paintings. Less known is that in 1911 Malevich designed the packaging and label for an Eau de Cologne called Severny, produced by Brocard & Co.

Manuale Typografico, 1817.

Maloof, Sam was an American furniture designer who is perhaps most famous for his sculptural yet also very ergonomic chair design. His favourite material was wood, that's why People magazine named him "The Hemingway of Hardwood".

Manuale Typografico also known as the Typographic Manual of Giambattista Bodoni is the greatest monument ever made to the art of printing from metal types. The two-volume Manual was released in 1817 in a print run of only 250 copies and includes 142 alphabets and the corresponding italics, script fonts and ornaments.

Mari, Enzo is an Italian artist and furniture designer. In 1974, he wrote the book "Autoprogettazione", which deals around the Do It Yourself construction of furniture.

Cadira Garriri, 1987 Javier Mariscal (1950). Donació Akaba SA, 1999. © Estudio Rafael Vargas.

Mariscal, Javier is a Spanish artist and designer who is probably best known for transforming Mickey Mouse into a chair.

Mason is a font from Jonathan Barnbrook who originally wanted to name it Manson, after the insane 1960s serial killer.

Masthead also known as imprint is a printed list of its owners, departments, officers and address details, published in a fixed position in each edition.

ℳason

Mason, designed by Jonathan Barnbrook in 1993. © Emigre.

World War II poster, 1941. Design: Herbert Matter.

Matter, Herbert was a Swiss-born American photographer and graphic designer. He is known for his pioneering use of photomontage in commercial art.

Matrix also known as Mat, was a copper mould of an image or a glyph. In phototypesetting, a matrix is a negative image of a character on a font disk.

MAYA is an acronym that stands for "Most Advanced, Yet Acceptable". It was coined by Raymond Loewy and became maxim for his design work.

McElroy, N. Hosler had been president of Procter & Gamble, an American consumer goods company. In 1931, McElroy was the first one to laid out the principles of modern brand management. He argued that companies should have a separate marketing team to each individual product brand.

Mead, Syd The US designer was initially asked to draw the flying police scooters for the movie Blade Runner, but the architectural background in his drawing prompted Ridley Scott to bring him on board for the designs of all the sets.

Meggs, Philip Baxter was one of the first educators to create an overview of the history of graphic design that went beyond the 19th and 20th centuries. His book History of Graphic Design is a definitive, standard read for the study of graphic design.

Mellor, David was an English designer and manufacturer who has been described as "Britain's greatest post-war product designer". He specialised in cutlery, to such an extent that he was often referred to as "the cutlery king".

Various objects of the Memphis Group.

Memphis Group, the was an Italian design and architecture group founded in Milan by Ettore Sottsass in 1981 that designed Postmodern furniture, fabrics, ceramics, glass and metal objects. The name was taken after the Bob Dylan song "Stuck Inside of Mobile with the Memphis Blues Again" which had been played repeatedly throughout the evening's meeting. The Memphis Group drew inspiration from movements such as Art Deco and Pop Art, including styles such as the 50s Kitsch and futuristic themes. The Memphis group's work often incorporated plastic laminate and was characterized by ephemeral design featuring colourful decoration and asymmetrical shapes.

Marcel Breuer's famous Wassily Chair redesign by Alessandro Mendini, 1983.

Mendini, Alessandro is an Italian designer and architect, who was one of the main personalities of the Radical design movement in the 1970s. With an ironic approach, he "remixed" legendary objects of other designers such as Joe Colombo's Universal Chair or Marcel Breuer's Wassily Chair.

Composed line with matrices and spacebands in a Linotype Machine.

Mergenthaler, Ottmar was a German inventor. He became famous through his invention of the linotype machine, that could easily and quickly set complete lines of type for use in printing presses. An operational Linotype machine is on display at the Baltimore Museum of Industry.

Meta Black
Meta Bold
Meta Medium
Meta Book
Meta Normal

Meta, designed by Erik Spiekermann and released in 1991.

Meta A humanist sans-serif typeface designed by Erik Spiekermann and released in 1991. It was intended to be a "complete antithesis of Helvetica", according to Spiekermann. Meta was comissioned by the German Federal Post Office in 1985. However, despite positive interest the Post Office decided not to implement the new typeface. At this time Meta was named PT 55 (regular weight) and PT 75 (bold).

Metamerism is a phenomenon that occurs when colours change when viewed in different light sources. Metamerism is almost inevitable with some colours and less of a problem with others. The colours that are most likely to have metameric problems include celadon, taupe, gray/blues, mauve, lilac, tan, and grays.

Michelin The "mascot" of French tire manufacturer has a name, it's Monsieur Bibendum. He's also a century old.

Michelin's Monsier Bibendum.

Milk Since the letters back then consisted of lead, the typesetter had to be very careful on cleanliness because the risk of lead poisoning, which can be fatal, was very large. Before this threat has been detected, many typesetters suffered at "lead poisoning". Many companies presented a free pint of milk or cocoa, which contained calcium, for their workers to prevent this.

Lounge Chair and Ottoman, 1956. Design: Charles and Ray Eames.

Miller, Herman is an American manufacturer of office and home furniture, founded in 1905. It is regarded as one of the first companies to produce modern furniture such as the Aeron chair, the Noguchi table, and the iconic Eames Lounge Chair.

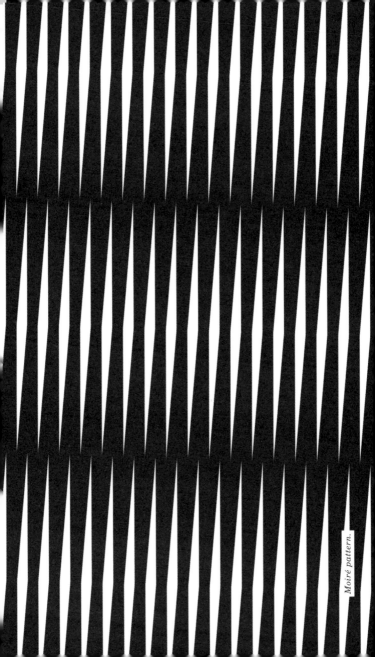

Moiré pattern.

Mistral is a casual script typeface designed by Roger Excoffon and released in 1953. It became a pretty popular typeface. Even the American rap group N.W.A used the font for their logo beginning with their 1988 album Straight Outta Compton.

Mnemonic In general, a mnemonic is a memory aid, such as an abbreviation, rhyme or mental image that helps to remember something.

Mock Up A recreation of the original printed material; could possibly contain instructions or directions.

Modulor, the is a stylised human figure developed by French architect Le Corbusier in 1943. The Modulor is a proportional system based on human measurements, the double unit, the Fibonacci numbers, and the golden ratio. It is intended to be used for the coordinated design of buildings, their contents, and their surroundings in a harmonious way. Le Corbusier was so proud of his creation that he even presented it to Albert Einstein who noticed: "It's a tool that makes the good easy and the bad difficult."

Moholy-Nagy, László was a hungarian painter and designer who became known for his innovative work in the fields of photography, typography, sculpture, painting, printmaking, and industrial design. In 1937 Moholy-Nagy founded the "New Bauhaus" in Chicago, which became the Institute of Design in 1944.

Moiré A repetitive pattern that causes interferences between a pattern in the data being printed and the screened dots.

Mollino, Carlo was an Italian designer of furniture, interiors, fashion, theatre and film sets. In collaboration with his friend Mario Damonte, Mollino even designed the aerodynamic "Damolnar Bisiluro" racing car which he actually drove at the Le Mans 24 hour race in 1954.

Carlo Mollino driving the Bisiluro.
© www.mondo-blogo.blogspot.de.

Monarch Paper size (216 × 179 mm) and envelope shape often used for personal stationery.

The "AD" monogram that Albrecht Dürer used as a signature.

Monogram A monogram is made by combining two or more letters or other graphemes to form a new symbol. Monograms first appeared on coins, as early as 350 BC, have been used as signatures by artists and craftsmen on paintings, sculptures and pieces of furniture.

Monospaced Font also called a fixed-pitch, fixed-width, or non-proportional font, is a font whose letters and characters have the same amount of horizontal space regardless of their shape or width. Examples of monospaced fonts: Courier, Lucida Console, Monaco, and Letter Gothic.

ABCDEFGHIJKLMNOPQ
RSTUVWXYZÀÁÉÎÕØÜa
bcdefghijklmnopqr
stuvwxyzàáéîõø&12
34567890($£€. , !?)

FF Isonorm Monospaced.

Monotype The Monotype System is a typesetting machine that was invented in 1897 by American engineer Tolbert Lanston. Unlike the Linotype typesetting machine, the operations set and casting are not combined in one machine.

Djinn Chair, 1965. Design: Oliver Morgue. © www.filmandfurniture.com.

Mont Blanc The number 4810 on the spring of Mont Blanc fountain pen indicates the height of the homonymous mountain.

Morrison, Jasper As a student the well-known product designer used assembled lamps out of items that were part of the equipment of Chemist's shops like rubber hoses, funnels and glass flasks.

Mourgue, Oliver is a French industrial designer best known as the designer of the futuristic bright red Djinn chairs used in the 1968 film "2001: A Space Odyssey".

kate moss

Logo for supermodel Kate Moss. Design: Peter Saville and Paul Barnes.

Moss, Kate is not only an iconic supermodel, she also has her won logo. The word mark, designed by Peter Saville and Paul Barnes, is based on "Brodovitch Albro", a typeface by Alexey Brodovitch, the legendary art director of women's fashion magazine Harper's Bazaar.

Mrs Eaves

Mrs Eaves, 2002. Design: Zuzana Licko for Emigre.

Mrs Eaves is a serif typeface created by Zuzana Licko in 1996. It is a variant of the typeface Baskerville, designed in 1757 by John Baskerville. Mrs Eaves is named after Sarah Eaves, a housekeeper and mistress who became John Baskerville's wife.

Mr. Yuk is a trademarked graphic image, used in the United States in labeling of substances that are poisonous if ingested. Mr. Yuk replaced the traditional skull and crossbones symbol, which was no longer appropriate for children, because it was mainly associated with pirates and buccaneers rather than with harmful substances.

Mr. Yuk, created by the Children's Hospital of Pittsburgh in 1971.

MTV The famous MTV logo was designed by Manhattan Design in 1981. They also conceived the adaptation of the MTV Moonman as the award for the annual MTV Video Music Awards.

MTV logo, 1981. Design: Manhattan Design.

Muji is a Japanese retail company founded in 1979, which sells household and consumer goods, characterised by its minimalistic design approach and recyclable materials. The name Muji is derived from the first part of "Mujirushi Ryohin", translated as "No Brand Quality Goods".

MUJI logo.

Mukai, Shutaro The Japanese design professor furnished his whole home with Eames's furniture for children, simply because the items suited well with his body size.

Multiple master fonts are adjustable PostScript fonts, offering design variations at the extremes of the design axis. This axis represents a given variable property for that font, such as: Weight (light vs. bold), Width (condensed vs. expanded), Optical size.

Falkland, 1964. Design: Bruno Munari.
© *www.ambientedirect.com.*

Munari, Bruno was an Italian designer, artist, and inventor. In the case of his suspended lamp Falkland from 1964, Bruno Munari inserted aluminium covered rings into an elastic hose – initially a lady's stocking.

Munsell colour system, the is a colour space that particularizes colours based on three dimensions: hue, value (lightness), and chroma (colour purity). It was developed by Professor Albert H. Munsell in the first decade of the 20th century.

Museum of Modern Art In 1932, the world-famous Museum of Modern Art established the world's first curatorial department devoted to architecture & design.

Muthesius, Eckart In 1927, architect Eckart Muthesius made the acquaintance of the Maharaja of Indore, Shir Yeswant Rao Holkar Bahadur, at a garden party in Oxford. A few weeks later Muthesius was commissioned to design the luxurious interior of the Maharaja's palace in the Art Deco idiom.

about "The Horse in Motion" starting in 1872, which should prove whether a galloping horse lifts all four hooves off the ground at one point in its sequence of motion. The results were a technical and conceptual breakthrough and it is believed that these pictures where the first stop-motion images ever.

Myriad The humanist sans-serif typeface made by Carol Twombly and Robert Slimbach in 1992 became primarily known as a corporate typeface of Apple in 2002 and was the first sans-serif typeface among the Adobe Originals. "Apple Myriad" replaced "Apple Garamond", which had been in use since 1984.

M Weight, the is the weight of 1,000 sheets of any given size of paper. The ream weight is the weight of 500 sheets.

"The Horse in Motion" by Eadweard Muybridge, 1878.

Muybridge, Eadweard was an English photographer pioneering in photographic studies of motion. Muybridge is known for his studies

NASA The round red, white and blue insignia, also known as the "meatball" was designed by employee James Modarelli in 1959. In 1975 NASA decided to design a more modern logo and the "worm", designed by Richard Danne and Bruce Blackburn, was introduced. That logo finally retired in 1992, and the classic meatball insignia has been reintroduced.

Top: NASA logotype ("worm"), 1974
Design: Danne & Blackburn.
Bottom: NASA Insignia ("meatball"),
1959. Design: James Modarelli.

National Medal of Arts On February 25, 2010, Milton Glaser was the first designer to receive the National Medal of Arts.

Negative Space The area of a page that doesn't contain images or words. Also known as white space.

Nelson, George was an American industrial designer who designed some of the 20th century's most iconic modernist furniture, for example his wall clocks. He is also known for several innovative concepts like the "storage wall" which followed the idea of utilizing the space in between walls.

Neruda, Pablo became known as a poet when he was 10 years old. He wrote in a variety of styles, including surrealist poems, historical epics, political manifestos, a prose autobiography, and several passionate love poems. He even paid tribute to the typographic arts in his joyous "Ode to Typography".

Pablo Neruda's signature.

Neurath, Otto was an Austrian philosopher of science, sociologist, and political economist. In 1923, he founded a new museum in Vienna for housing and city planning which he later named "Gesellschafts- und Wirtschaftsmuseum" (Social and economic museum). To make the museum understandable for everybody, Neurath worked on graphic design and visual education. With the help of illustrator Gerd Arntz and Marie Reidemeister (his wife), they created Isotype, a "universal" picture language.

ABCDEFGHIJKKLMM
NOPQQQRSTUVWWXYZ
aabcdefgghijkklmnopqrstuuvwxyz
11223344556677889900

Neutraface, 2002. Design: Christian Schwartz. Released by House Industries.

Neutraface The geometric sans-serif typeface was inspired by the

Marc Newson, Lockheed Lounge. Photography: Clint Blowers. © Phillips.

architecture of the Austrian architect Richard Neutra. He often used numbers and letters in his drawings that inspired House Industries to design a whole font family. From these templates, Christian Schwartz generated the complete alphabet.

New Bauhaus, the is a school of design founded in 1937 in Chicago by László Moholy-Nagy, a former Bauhaus teacher. The philosophy of the school basically didn't change and kept focusing on systemic, human-centered design. In 1944, the New Bauhaus became part of the Illinois Institute of Technology and was renamed Institute of Design. Prominent alumni included Ivan Chermayeff, Louis Sauer and Robert Brownjohn.

The Nike Swoosh, designed by Carolyn Davidson in 1971 and used by Nike, Inc.

Newson, Marc In the video clip for her single "Rain", Madonna undulates on a "Lockheed Lounge" chaise-longue which was made by the Australian designer in 1986.

Newspaper The five highest-circulation newspapers in the world are distributed in Japan.

Newspaper format (mm)

Broadsheet	749 × 597
Nordisch	570 × 400
Rhenish	350 × 520
Swiss (NZZ)	475 × 320
Berliner	470 × 315
Tabloid	430 × 280

NeXT is the name of the company Steve Jobs founded in 1998 after leaving Apple. Less know is that the World's first web server ran a NeXT system.

Nike The Swoosh, also known as the logo of sportswear and apparel company Nike, was originally designed by the graphic design student Carolyn Davidson for only $35.

Logo of the Federal Design Improvement Program. Design: John Massey.

Nixon, Richard In May 1974, the US Government, under the leadership of Richard Nixon, started the Federal Design Improvement Program. The Program set out to improve the quality of visual communications and the ability of governmental representations to communicate effectively to citizens.

Noguchi table. Design: Isamo Noguchi. © www.ambientedirect.com.

Noguchi, Isamu was an American landscape architect whose artistic career spanned six decades, from the 1920s onward. In 1947, Noguchi began a collaboration with the Herman Miller company, when he joined with George Nelson, Paul László and Charles Eames to produce a catalog containing what is often considered to be the most influential body of modern furniture ever produced, including the iconic Noguchi table which remains in production today.

No Logo is a book by the Canadian author Naomi Klein which became one of the most influential books about the alter-globalization movement. No Logo: Taking Aim at the Brand Bullies deals with the negative effects of brand-oriented corporate activity of global players like Nike, The Gap, Shell, McDonald's, and Microsoft.

the nickname for the blank boxes that are shown when a computer or site lacks font support for a particular character.

N. W. Ayer & Son called itself the oldest advertising agency in the US. It was found in Philadelphia in 1869.

No More T☐fu

Noto font family, 2016.

Noto is a font family which aims to support more than 800 languages included in the Unicode Consortium standard. Noto was created by Monotype on behalf of Google. The name Noto is derived from the idea to see "No More Tofu"–tofu being

Oblique

Oxymoron

Oblique A Roman typeface which slants to the right. Often confused with italics.

Octavo Book whose signatures consist of a sheet of paper folded three times, generating 16-page signatures. This is generally done for small-sized books, such as paperbacks.

```
ABCDEFGHIJKLMNOP
QRSTUVWXYZÀÅÉÎÕØ
abcdefghijklmnop
qrstuvwxyzàå&123
4567890($£€.¬!?)
```

OCR-A, American Type Founders, 1968.

OCR-A is a monospace font that arose in the early days of computer optical character recognition when there was a need for a font that could be recognized not only by the computers of that day, but also by humans. It was produced by the American Type Founders in 1968. OCR-A figures are still in use today on cheques and credit cards.

```
ABCDEFGHIJKLMNO
PQRSTUVWXYZßØÜä
bcdefghijklmnop
qrstuvwxyz&1234
567890($£.,!?)
```

OCR-B, Adrian Frutiger, 1968.

OCR-B is a monospace font developed in 1968 by Adrian Frutiger. He was commissioned by the European Computer Manufacturers Association (ECMA) to design a font in the tradition of OCR-A but that is way easier for the human eye to read and that has a less technical look.

Ogilvy, David was a trained chef in the first place. At the age of 37 years he founded the now world famous agency Ogilvy & Mather.

OK The most used word in the world is "ok", followed by the word "Cola".

OK sheet The final colour inking sheet that is signed off by the customer before the production starts to print.

Old German paper sizes (mm)

Folio	210 × 330
Quart	225 × 285
Oktav	142,5 × 225
Brief	270 × 420
Kanzlei	330 × 420
Propatria	340 × 430
Groß Patria	360 × 450
Bischof	380 × 480
Löwen	400 × 500
Median 1	420 × 530
Klein Median	440 × 560
Post	460 × 560
Median 2	460 × 590
Klein Royal	480 × 640
Lexikon	500 × 650
Super Royal	500 × 680
Imperial	570 × 780

Old Style A style of type characterized by slight contrast between light and heavy strokes and slanting serif.

Olivetti is an Italian manufacturer of typewriters and computers, who was famous for the attention it gave to their product designers, such as Mario Bellini or Ettore Sottsass. Olivetti's "Programma 101", made in 1964, is considered the first commercial "desktop computer".

Olivetti's Programma 101 from 1964.
© Museo nazionale della scienza e
della tecnologia Leonardo da Vinci.

Onionskin is a thin, light-weight, often translucent paper.

Open Type A font format created by Adobe Systems and Microsoft. Open Type fonts can include a set of glyphs defined as True Type or Type 1.

Optical character recognition is a mechanical or electronic recognition of images of typed, handwritten or printed text by a computer, whether from a scanned document, a photo of a document etc.

Orphan An orphan is a paragraph-opening line that appears by itself at the bottom of a page or column, thus separated from the rest of the text.

Ortelius World Map Typvs Orbis
Terrarvm, 1570.

Ortelius, Abraham was a Flemish cartographer and geographer. His book "Theatrum Orbis Terrarum", meaning "Theatre of the World", released in 1570, is considered to be the first true modern atlas.

Oxford Comma The Oxford comma is an optional comma before the word "and" at the end of a list: We sell books, videos, and magazines. It's known as the Oxford comma because it was traditionally used by printers, readers, and editors at Oxford University Press. It is also known as the "serial comma".

Oxymoron An oxymoron is a figure of speech that juxtaposes elements that appear to be contradictory, but which contain a hidden point. For example: Dark light, Living Dead or Science Fiction.

P

P22 Type Foundry is a digital type foundry from Buffalo, New York that specializes in historical letterforms inspired by art, history, and science that have never been available previously in digital format. The foundry was born when one of the founders Richard Kegler digitized Marcel Duchamp's handwriting for a masters thesis.

Palaeography The study of ancient and historical handwriting so that they may be dated, read, etc., and may serve as historical and literary sources.

ABCDEFGHIJKLMN
OPQRSTUVWXYZÀ
ÅÉÎÕabcdefghijklmn
opqrstuvwxyzàåéîõø
&1234567890($£€.,!?)

Palatino, 1949. Design: Hermann Zapf.

Palatino is the name of an old-style serif typeface made by Hermann Zapf. The first use took place in Goethe's "The Three Reverences" printed by the font foundry D. Stempel in 1949. The publication was only available in a limited edition of 1,000 numbered copies. Typography enthusiasts pay a small fortune for the book, which is set in an early version of Palatino.

Palmer, Volney was probably the first person to open an advertising agency in Philadelphia in 1841. It is said that he even created the term "advertising agency".

Pangram A pangram or holoalphabetic sentence for a given alphabet is a sentence using every letter of the alphabet at least once. A pangram has been used to display typefaces, test equipment, and develop skills in handwriting, calligraphy, and keyboarding. The perfect pangram can be considered an anagram of the alphabet; it is the shortest possible pangram. An example is the phrase "Cwm fjord bank glyphs vext quiz" (cwm, a loan word from Welsh, means a steep-sided valley, particularly in Wales). The most famous English pangram is "The quick brown fox jumps over the lazy dog."

Pantograph.

Pantograph A mechanical instrument used to copy an image to a different scale. The pantograph is made of hinged and jointed rods. The first pantograph was constructed in 1603 by Christoph Scheiner.

Panton, Verner created the first-ever Vitra chair. The world-famous "Panton Chair" did go into production in 1967 and was available in different colours. Panton claimed that: "One sits more comfortable on a colour one likes".

Papanek, Victor Joseph was a designer who became a strong advocate of the socially and ecologically responsible design of products. He wrote: "Much recent design has satisfied only evanescent wants and desires, while the genuine needs of man have often been neglected by the designer."

Paper A sheet of paper can not be folded in half more than nine times.

Papyrus Typeface, 1983. Design: Chris Costello.

Papyrus is a handwritten, calligraphy inspired font from Chris Costello. Ten type companies refused to purchase Papyrus, before it was finally bought by Letraset.

Parent sheet Any sheet larger than 27.9 × 43 cm or DIN A3.

"Tongue and Lip Design" logo, 1971. Design: John Pasche.

Pasche, John is a graphic designer, most known for designing the iconic "Tongue and Lip Design" logo for The Rolling Stones in 1971, which was originally reproduced on the Sticky Fingers album. The logo exaggerates Jagger's mouth features and was probably one of the first logo of rock brand marketing. After designing the logo, Pasche ended up working for the Stones from 1971 to 1974.

Password The most used password is "123456", followed by "qwerty" or even "password".

Patria Max Bill saw himself as an architect, but was also a designer, painter and sculptor. In 1944 Bill even designed a typewriter model for the Swiss brand "Patria". It was his first design that went into serial production. The revision of the typewriter was Max Bill's breakthrough as a product designer. The "Patria" was still widespread, until the 90s.

Playboy Logo. Design: Arthur Paul.

Paul, Arthur Arthur "Art" Paul is an American Art Director of Playboy magazine. He also designed the iconic rabbit-head logo. It was developed by Paul for Playboy's second issue. He supposedly sketched the logo in about an hour.

"Orange Slice Chair", 1960. Design: Pierre Paulin. © Rama.

Paulin, Pierre was a French furniture and interior designer. He be-

122

came most famous for his chair designs including the famous Mushroom chair (1959), the Ribbon chair (1966) and the iconic Tongue chair (1968). His method using metallic frames covered with stretch materials has influenced a lot of designers.

PDF Stands for Portable Document Format, developed by Adobe Systems. The program, Adobe Acrobat serves as a universal browser. Files can be downloaded over the web and viewed page by page, provided the user's computer has installed the application.

Peace Symbol, 1958. Design: Gerald Holtom.

Peace Symbol, the was designed by Gerald Holtom in 1958 for the Campaign for Nuclear Disarmament has become a universal symbol for peace. It is based on the semaphore symbols for "N" for Nuclear (two flags held 45 degrees down on both sides, forming the triangle at the bottom) and "D" for Disarmament (two flags, one above the head and one at the feet, forming the vertical line).

Pencil of Nature, the was the first commercially published book illustrated with photographs. Written by William Henry Fox Talbot in 1844, it was wholly executed by the

new art of Photogenic Drawing. Since people were still unfamiliar with photography, Talbot included the following notice into his book: "The plates of the present work are impressed by the agency of Light alone, without any aid from the artist's pencil. They are the sun-pictures themselves, and not, as some persons have imagined, engravings in imitation."

Cover of The Pencil of Nature, 1844.

Penny Black, the was the world's first adhesive stamp used by a public postal system. It was printed in black ink and features a profile of Queen Victoria.

Perri, Dan was a film and television title sequence designer who has created main titles for more than 400 film and television projects, including Star Wars, Raging Bull and Taxi Driver.

Perriand, Charlotte was a French furniture designer and architect. At the beginning of her career she applied for work at the famous Le Corbusier's studio in 1927. At first she was famously rejected with the reply "We don't embroider cushions here". In the meantime Perriand re-created her appartment, which included a bar made of aluminium glass and chrome, for the "Salon d'Automne". This work caught the attention of Le Corbusier's partner Pierre Jeanneret, convincing Corbusier to offer her a job.

World's first postal stamp: the Penny Black, Great Britain, 1840.

Peru is the name of the smallest book in the world. It measures 0.3 by 1.0 millimetres and contains the six verses of the Peruvian National Anthem.

Pesce, Gaetano is an Italian architect and a leading figure in contemporary industrial design. His work is characterized by an innovative use of colours, materials and production processes. His famous chair "Nobody's Perfect" is manufactured completely by hand. Thus each chair is different and the person who physically produces it becomes part of the design process.

Pfund, Roger is a Swiss graphic designer and artist who is probably best known for designing Switzerland's bank notes, the last version of the French franc, as well as a series of the Euro.

The phenakistoscope. Picture taken from McLean's Optical Illusions or Magic Panorama disc, 1833.

Phénakisticope, the was the first animation device to create an illusion of motion. It was invented by Belgian physicist Joseph Plateau. In 1833 it became a predecessor for the future motion picture and film industry.

Swiss Commemorative Coin, 2005. Design: Roger Pfund.

Phototypesetting is the automatic production of typesetting by photographic means. The final good is a film or photographic paper, which is used for the copy of the printing forms. The origins of phototypesetting go back to the 19th century. But only in the middle of the 20th century these technique found their way into the printing industry.

Pica is the unit of measurement for type. Commonly used for typewriters. The contemporary computer pica is 1/72 of the International foot of 1959, 4.233 mm or 0.166 in.

Pictogram for woman and man.

Pictogram A pictogram is an image that represents a specific object. As a "visible language" it is more or less understood regardless of one's native language or educational background.

Pi font A typeface that contains characters that are not usually included in a font, such as mathematical signs.

Pigsty In 1968, Walter Gropius made a bet with the entrepreneur Philip Rosenthal to the effect that he believed a certain dinner service manufactured by Rosenthal would not sell in the United States. As his assumption turned out to be false, to pay off his debt Gropius together with two of his assistants designed for the Rosenthal company premises in Selb, the new home for a pig named Roro.

Pilcrow, the (¶) is also called the paragraph mark, paragraph sign, paraph, alinea (Latin: alinea, "off

the line"), or blind P. It is a typographical character for individual paragraphs and can be used for separate paragraphs or to designate a new paragraph in one long piece of copy, as Eric Gill did in his 1930s book, An Essay on Typography.

Cipe Pineles at Condé Nast. © Thomas Golden.

Pineles, Cipe was an Austrian designer and art director. She became the first autonomous woman art director of a mass-market American publication, the Glamour. She was also the first woman to be asked to join the all-male New York Art Directors Club and later their Hall of Fame.

Pioneer plaque, the was the first pictorial message sent into space. The plaques, entirely made of gold-anodized aluminium, were attached to the antenna of Pioneer 10 and 11 spacecraft and showed the nude figures of a human male and female along with varied symbols that provided information about the origin of the spacecraft. They were both designed by Carl Sagan and Frank Drake in 1972.

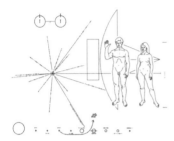

Illustration on the Pioneer plaque.

Pixel Acronym of Picture Element. A Pixel is the basic unit of colour on a computer display or in a digital image.

Poster design by Lucian Bernhard.

Plakatstil also known as Sachplakat (object poster), was an early style of poster art in Germany in the 1900s, supported by artists like Ludwig Hohlwein, Lucian Bernhard, Julius Klinger, Paul Scheurich, and Otto Baumberger. The characteristics of this poster style are bold eye-catching lettering with flat colours and simplified illustrations of objects.

Plantin
Times New Roman

Plantin, 1913 versus Times New Roman, 1932.

Plantin is an old-style serif typeface named after the printer Christophe Plantin. Plantin, designed by Robert Granjon, was based on the older typeface Gros Cicero. Plantin is one of the typefaces that influenced the creation of the well-known Times New Roman in the 1930s.

Garamond Matrices created by Jean Jannon around 1640. © ActuaLitté.

Plantin-Moretus Museum, the is a museum in Antwerp, Belgium that possesses the two oldest surviving printing presses in the world and complete sets of dies and matrices of the original Garamond typeface.

PNG Portable Network Graphics format, usually pronounced "ping", is used for lossless compression. The PNG format displays images without jagged edges while keeping file sizes rather small for usage on the web.

Point The basic unit of typographic measure. Type size and line spacing are both expressed in terms of points. Over the centuries, various point systems have been devised, including the Didot, pica, and the Anglo-Saxon systems.

Superleggera, 1957. Design: Gio Ponti. © Cassina.

Ponti, Gio To illustrate how lightweight and sturdy his chair Superleggera (1957) was, Gio Ponti threw the chair out of a fourth floor window unto a street, where it hit the ground without breaking apart.

Porsche, Ferdinand Alexander In 1957 Porsche was expelled at Ulm School of Design after completing the basic course. On the recommendations of Hans Gugelot, the young designer had come to the HfG and taken part in the 101 course taught by Tomás Maldonado. Maldonado, who was also principal of the HfG at the time "out of the blue revealed to Porsche that he would not be allowed to continue his studies." "He did not give a reason." Porsche could not recall having done anything to justify his expulsion, writes Uta Brandes in her monograph on Porsche.

Potaka is the first ever sentence based easy bangla programming language. It was created by Ikrum Hossain, a software engineer.

PPI Measurement of the resolution of a computer display. PPI stands for Pixels Per Inch.

Preetorius, Emil (1883–1973) was a German illustrator and graphic artist. He is also one of the most important stage designers of the first half of the 20th century. In 1909 he founded the School of Illustration and Book Trade in Munich, together with Paul Renner.

Primary colours are put together to produce the full range of other colours(non-primary colours), within a colour model. Primary colours for the additive colour model is red, green, and blue. Primary colours for the subtractive colour model is cyan, magenta, and yellow.

Printer's Mark of Peter Schöffer at the end of "Valerius Maximus", 1471.

Printer's Devil A Printer's Devil was a young apprenticeship who worked in a printer's office and performed several tasks, such as mixing ink, fetching type or washing the black ink off the ink rollers. There are several theories of the phrase's origin: English tradition for example refers to the assistant of the first printer and book publisher, William Caxton, whose assistant was named "Deville", which over time evolved to "devil".

Printer's mark is a symbol identifying a particular printer, first used by the Venetian printer Aldus Manutius as his mark in 1502.

ABCDEFGHIJKLMNO
PQRSTUVWXYZÀÁÉ
ÎÕØÜabcdefghijklmn
opqrstuvwxyzàáéîõøü
&1234567890($£€.,!?)

*Proforma, 1988. Design: Petr van
Blokland.*

Proforma is a Roman typeface created by Petr van Blokland, a dutch type and graphic designer, in the mid-1980s for the Danish typesetting company Purup. In 1995 Proforma was nominated – as the first typeface ever – for the Rotterdam Design Award.

Prouvé, Jean was a French metal worker, self-taught architect and designer. In 1971, Prouvé was the president of the Jury for the design of the Centre Pompidou in Paris. Along with fellow jury member Philip Johnson, he played a very important role for the choice of the winning project by Richard Rogers and Renzo Piano.

Puiforcat, Jean was a French silversmith, sculptor and designer who could name the famous artist Andy Warhol a collector of his work. Warhol acquired Puiforcat silverware while visiting Paris in the 1970s. After Warhol's dead in 1987, the collection was sold at Sotheby's for $451,000.

Push Pin Studios is a graphic design studio founded in New York City in 1954 by Cooper Union graduates Reynold Ruffins, Edward So-

rel, Seymour Chwast, and Milton Glaser. The bi-monthly publication "The Push Pin Graphic" was a product of their collaboration.

Tea service, 1972. Design: Jean Puiforcat in 1972. © Heinz Thate.

Q The letter Q appears in German texts only with a chance of 0.02 percent.

Quarter Binding A type of bookbinding in which the spine is covered in a different and generally fancier material than the covers.

Quarto A book whose signatures consist of a sheet of paper twice, creating an 8-page signature, usually done for medium-sized books.

Quasar and his family in one of his inflatable living rooms, 1966.

Quasar Better known as Nguyen Manhkhan'n is a Vietnamese designer who works in France. He was a pioneer of inflatable furniture, like his inflatable armchairs "Apollo" and "Venus". He even designed an inflatable living room in 1966. In 1967/68, he developed the very first line of inflatable furniture, the collection "Aerospace" which instantly became a standard of design.

Quire A quire of paper is a measure of paper quantity. The usual meaning is 25 sheets of the same size and quality: 1/20 of a ream of 500 sheets. Quires of 25 sheets are often used for machine-made paper, while quires of 24 sheets are often used for handmade or specialised paper of 480-sheet reams. As an old UK and US measure, a quire was originally 24 sheets. Quires of 15 or 20 sheets have also been in use, depending on the type of paper.

Quistgaard, Jens was a Danish designer and sculptor whose work for the American company "Dansk Designs" in the 1950s quickly became synonymous with Scandinavian Design. He was hugely productive and designed more than 4,000 products.

QWERTY describes the standard English language typewriter keyboard layout with the characters q, w, e, r, t, and y positioned on the top row of the keyboard.

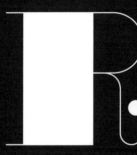

Peter Raacke

Gordon Russell

Raacke, Peter is not only know for his cutlery series mono-a, he also advertised the slogan "Duracell – the endurance cell." in 1973.

Race, Ernest was a British product designer who created some of the most iconic designs of the post-war era, including the Antelope and BA3 chair. The BA3 chair was made of re-cast aluminium from redundant British fighter planes, while the upholstery fabric was made out of parachute silk.

Radio Nurse In 1937, Japanese-American sculptor Isamu Noguchi created the iconic "Radio Nurse" for the Zenith Radio Corporation. It was originally commissioned by the firm's president in order to monitor his daughter on his yacht. The Radio Nurse's shape suggests both traditional Japanese Kendo masks and American machine age sculpture of the 1930s. This product is very rare today, since many patriotic parents smashed their Radio's after the Japanese attack on Pearl Harbour.

RAF The commercial artist Holm of Czettritz was asked by Andreas Baader, to revise the logo of the RAF.

Rainbow Fountain Technique of putting ink colours next to each other in the same ink fountain and oscillating the ink rollers to make the colours merge where they meet, producing a rainbow effect.

RAL In 1927 the German Reichs-Ausschuß für Lieferbedingungen und Gütesicherung (Imperial Commission for Delivery Terms and Quality Assurance) invented a collection of forty colours under the name of RAL 840. Prior to that date manufacturers and customers had to exchange samples to describe a tint. From then on they would rely on numbers. RAL 3000 for example is the classic fire engine red.

Rambow, Gunter The renowned graphic artist created a book that contains nothing but photographs of vaginas. This highly acclaimed publication entitled "Doris" was published in 1970 by the März publishing house.

Good design is innovative

Good design makes a product useful

Good design is aesthetic

Good design makes a product understandable

Good design is unobtrusive

Good design is honest

Good design is long-lasting

Good design is thorough down to the last detail

Good design is environmentally friendly

Good design is as little as possible

Dieter Rams: Ten Principles of "Good Design".

Rams, Dieter is a German industrial designer who is probably best know for his work for Braun and

Radio Nurse, 1937. Design: Isamu Noguchi.

Paul Rand's popular Eye-Bee-M Rebus poster, 1981. © IBM.

Vitsœ. His belief in "less but better" influenced the design of many products and concluded in his Ten Principles of "Good Design", which are still referential.

NeXT Logo, 1986. Design: Paul Rand.

Rand, Paul was an American art director and graphic designer, best known for his corporate logo designs for IBM, UPS and Enron. In 1986, he was hired by Steve Jobs to design the brand identity for NeXT Computer, costing a price of $100,000.

Ray Ban Turned into a design icon by the Blues Brothers, the Classic Wayfarer model was designed by the American Ray Stegman.

Ray Gun was an American alternative Rock and Roll Magazine. It was founded by art director David Carson in 1992. Ray Gun pushed boundaries of experimental magazine typographic design and once published an interview entirely in the symbol font Zapf Dingbats.

Reading Speed The normal reading speed is about 240 words per minute, which is about the page of a paperback.

Rearview Mirror The career of 23-year-old German industrial designer Richard Sapper began with the design of a Rearview Mirror of the Mercedes-Benz 300 SL Roadster in 1956.

Rearview Mirror, Mercedes-Benz 300 SL Roadster, 1956. © Richard Sapper.

Rebus A representation of words in the form of pictures or symbols. The Rebus helped developing a phonetic alphabet starting in Egyptian hieroglyphics, used at Abydos in Egypt as early as 3400 BC.

Red Cross, Islamic Crescent, Red Diamond.

Red Cross The Red Cross logo was designed by Henri Dunant, the founder of the Red Cross, and the first recipient of the Nobel Peace Prize, in 1863. The emblem of a red cross with arms of equal length on a white background is the visible sign of protection under the 1949 Geneva Conventions. Those that decline the cross symbol because of semantic confusion use the Red Crescent, the Red Diamond or the Red Star of David.

Red-green colour blindness Eight percent of men and 0.5 percent of women are suffering from a red-green colour blindness.

Reed, Ethel was an internationally recognized graphic design artist. In 1894, at the age of twenty-one, she found herself being described in the press as the foremost woman graphic artist in America.

Ethel Reed, Albert Morris Bagby's New Novel "Miss Träumerei" poster, 1895.

Reich, Lilly was a German textile and furniture designer and close collaborator with Ludwig Mies van der Rohe. It is less known that she co-designed the famous Barcelona Chair in 1929.

Reichel, Hans is the inventor of several famous typefaces like FF Dax, FF Barmeno or FF Sari. Less known is that he also was a guitarist and even built his own instruments. His Daxophone for example is a single wooden blade fixed in a block containing a contact microphone, which is played mostly with a bow.

A variety of Daxophone tongues, invented by Hans Reichel in the 1980s.

Reid, Jamie was the Graphic Artist of the Sex Pistols and best known as the man who sealed the Queen's lips with a safety pin. "God Save The Queen" (Cecil Beaton photograph of Queen Elizabeth II), with an added safety pin through her nose and swastikas in her eyes, indicated by Sean O'Hagan of The Observer as "the single most iconic image of the punk era."

Logo for Reuters, now Thomson Reuters, 1965. Design: Alan Fletcher.

Reuters was an international news agency. The idea for the design of the logo by Alan Fletcher was born out of the holes punched out of the ticker tape which originally were used to transmit information. The logotype remained in use in its original form until 1996.

RGB stands for Red, Green, Blue and is the colour model used to project colour on a computer monitor.

By combining these three colours, a large percentage of the visible colour spectrum can be represented.

Gerrit Rietveld's Red and Blue chair, 1917.

Rietveld, Gerrit Thomas was an iconic furniture designer and architect of Dutch origin and one of the main members of the artistic movement called De Stijl. He is probably best known for his Red and Blue Chair from 1917.

Rimowa The extremely light aluminium suitcase called Topas was especially created for air travel. In order to enhance its stability, Junior Director Richard Morszeck gave the suitcase rows of grooves on the sides. He had the JU 52 airplane in mind, whose iron cladding had a similar structure.

Risom, Jens is a Danish American furniture designer who was one of the first to introduce Scandinavian design in the United States in the 1950s. Less known is that one of his executive office chairs became famous when Lyndon B. Johnson,

36th President of the US, chose to use it in the Oval Office.

River In typography, rivers, or rivers of white, are gaps in typesetting, which appear to run through a paragraph of text, due to a coincidental alignment of spaces.

Rodchenko and his wife Varvara Stepanova, 1920.

Rodchenko, Alexander was an artist and graphic designer and one of the founders of Russian constructivism. A lot of graphic designers of the 20th century were influenced by his pioneering, including the cover art for a number of music albums like Franz Ferdinand's "You Could Have It So Much Better".

Rohde, Gilbert was an American furniture and industrial designer who introduced the furniture manufacturer Hermann Miller to modern design. Rohde also established the earliest example of a systems approach to office furniture, called Executive Office Group (EOG) line, launched in 1942 by Herman Miller.

Rohe, Mies van der emigrated to the United States in 1938. When the famous architect traveled from Chicago to Germany to finish his emigration plans, he was immediately interrogated by the Gestapo. Mies realized he was in danger and left Berlin immediately. Herbert Hirche, the last remaining staffer in Mies' Berlin office, accompanied him to the station.

Rolling Stones, the Their famous album cover for Sticky Fingers was actually designed by Andy Warhol. It pictures a close-up of a male's crotch dressed in Jeans that included a real zipper. Once you open the record sleeve it reveals a photograph of a pair of underpants bearing the stamp: "Andy Warhol: This photograph may not be … etc."

Roman Type Generic term used to refer to upright characters, as opposed to slanted ones (italics).

AbCdeFgHi jKlmNopqRs TuVwXyZ

Hollandsche Mediæval, 1912. Design: Sjoerd de Roos.

Roos, Sjoerd Hendrik de was a Dutch type designer, book cover designer and visual artist. Roos is considered to be Holland's first professional type designer when he designed the serif typeface Hollandsche Mediæval in 1912, the first Dutch made typeface for 150 years.

Rosetta Stone, the was the first Ancient Egyptian bilingual text recovered in modern times. The stone featured the same text in three different scripts: Demotic, Greek, and Egyptian hieroglyphs. The Rosetta stone made it possible to decipher the previously untranslated hieroglyphic language. The stone was rediscovered in July 1799 in Egypt by a soldier named Pierre-François Bouchard.

The Rosetta Stone.

Rossum, Just van is a Dutch typeface designer and computer programmer, who designed the first dynamically generated typeface, which modified letterforms on the fly, called Beowulf. In addition his FF Justlefthand was the first digital handwriting font ever.

Rotunda is a specific Italian medieval blackletter script, which was used mainly in southern Europe. It derived from the Italian Bolognese script

The Roundel.

Roundel, the The London Underground logo, know as the Roundel is one of the most recognised and imitated logos in the world. In 1913 Frank Pick, British transport administrator, commissioned Edward Johnston to design a company typeface. In 1915 Johnston also reworked the originally red disc from 1908.

Rügerin, Anna was the very first woman to ever add her name to the colophon of a printed book. She published two books in the folio format in 1484 in the city of Augsburg, Germany.

Rupee There are 14 different fonts printed on an Indian Rupee bill.

Russell, Gordon was an English product designer and craftsman. During World War II he was one of the main figures in developing utility furniture, such as a dressing table. He also became the first chairman of the Crafts Council.

S

Saarinen, Eero

Saarinen, Eero was an industrial designer, who is best known for his neofuturistic style. His noted "Tulip chair" is often considered as "space age design". Less known is that the Finnish-American architect had a close relationship with fellow students Charles and Ray Eames, why he named his son Eames.

Tulip chair, 1956. Design: Eero Saarinen.

Saatchi & Saatchi is a global communications and advertising agency network that launched with a fearless full-page ad in the Sunday Times in 1970.

Sabon is an old-style serif typeface designed by the German-born typographer Jan Tschichold. Sabon is based on types by Claude Garamond and features 6 weights. The typeface's name pays tribute to the man who bought up Helvetica's estate after his death. This man was Jacques Sabon, a French punchcutter and typefounder.

Sabon

Sabon Regular, 1964. Design: Jan Tschichold.

Sacco was designed by Piero Gatti, Cesare Paolini and Franco Teodoro in 1968. The beanbag chair was usually intended to be filled with water, which would have made it impossible to carry it around. Thus the creators opted for the solution that applies to this day: The filling consists of polystyrene balls.

Sacco Chair, 1968. Design: Piero Gatti, Cesare Paolini and Franco Teodoro. © www.ambientedirect.com.

Sagmeister, Stefan is supposedly best known for the AIGA Detroit poster design from 1999, for which Sagmeister carved the program information onto his body.

Saladino, Gaspar was an American letterer and logo designer who worked for more than 50 years in the comic book industry. He made the logos for DC Comic's Vigilante

140

Swamp Thing, House of Mystery, and Adam Strange, among others.

TO BE SOLD BY AUCTION WITHOUT RESERVE; HOUSEHOLD FURNITURE PLATE, GLASS, AND OTHER EFFECTS.

Two-line great Primer Sans-serif by Vincent Figgins, 1832.

Sans-Serif The term sans-serif was first employed in 1832 by Vincent Figgins, when he created "Two-line great Primer Sans-serif". Figgins was a British punchcutter and type-founder. His most influential typeface was Ionic, created in 1821. It became the model for many twentieth century newspaper typefaces.

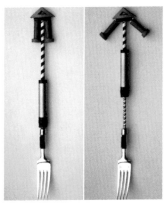

Auto-rotating spaghetti fork, 1981.
© Richard Sapper.

Sapper, Richard Besides being one of the most famous industrial designer of his generation, Richard Sapper also created the auto-rotat-ing spaghetti fork in 1981, during a design conference called "Essen und Ritual" organized by Alessi at the IDZ Berlin. This fork was designed to allow the distracted German tourist to eat spaghetti while watching TV. It works along the lines of the humming top reeling-in the noodles when pressed down and features a post-modernist accessory at the top.

Sasson, Steve In 1975 the Kodak engineer invented the world's first digital camera. It was the size of a toaster, and captured black and white images that were stored on cassette tape, taking 23 seconds to write.

World's First Digital Camera, 1975. Photo Copyright © 2016 Kodak. Used with permission.

Savignac, Raymond was a French graphic artist famous for his commercial posters who started designing under the direction of Cassandre. His greatest success were the posters for Yoplait yogurt.

Saville, Peter In 1987, British designer Peter Saville was desperately in need for a visual idea. He was sitting in his car when a brown leaf fell upon its hood. He immediately used this motif for the New Order CD "True Faith".

Sawyer, Tom The novel published in 1876, by the American author Mark Twain was the first which was typed on a typewriter.

Scala In 1988 Martin Majoor started working as a graphic designer for the Vredenburg Music Centre in Utrecht. The design department of this venue was one of the first in the Netherlands to use an Apple Macintosh computer. Unfortunately there were only 16 typefaces available, none with features like old style figures or ligatures. So Majoor decided to make his own typeface and named it after the "La Scala opera house" in Milan, referring to the concert hall Vredenburg.

Scala Sans

FF Scala, 1991. Design: Martin Majoor.

Scarpa, Carlo was an Italian architect and furniture designer who has been dedicated with a composition for orchestra in microintervals, called "A Carlo Scarpa, Architetto, Ai suoi infiniti possibili". It was made by the Italian composer Luigi Nono in 1984.

Schawinsky, Alexander known as Xanti Schawinsky was a Swiss designer and artist who studied at the famous Bauhaus school. His work was very versatile and especially his posters and product designs have become classics of commercial design of the 1930s.

Schelter & Giesecke was a German type foundry and manufacturer of printing presses. The foundry is considered to be one of the first to offer sans-serif typeface with lowercase letters as early as 1825.

schreIBMaschinen

Michael Schirner for IBM. © IBM.

Schirner, Michael By setting the word "Schreibmaschinen" in lowercase typewriter type and the letters IBM in uppercase, Michael Schirner brought out more clearly the semantic significance of the arrangement. The visual was actually inspired by a poster from 1953, designed by Anton Stankowski, who printed within the word the letters IBM in bold.

Schlemmer, Oskar was a German artist, sculptor, designer and choreographer associated with the Bauhaus school. In 2000, his daughter Ute J. Schlemmer, who purported that she owns the painting "Bauhaus Stairway", obtained a court order to hold it for further investigation while it was on temporary loan from the Museum of Modern Art in New York to the Neue Nationalgalerie in Berlin. Before the injunction was served on the Neue Nationalgalerie, "Bauhaus Stairway" had already been packed and shipped to New York.

Schütte-Lihotzky, Margarete was the first female Austrian architect and an activist in the Nazi resistance movement. She is mostly remembered today for designing the so-called Frankfurt Kitchen, made to enable efficient work and to be built at low cost.

Senftenberg Egg, 1968. Design: Peter Ghyczy. © Skjerven Group GmbH.

Oskar Schlemmer's "Bauhaustreppe", 1981.

Screen Printing Technique of printing by using a squeegee to force ink through an assembly of mesh fabric and a stencil.

Semiotics is the study of signs and symbols and sign processes. This also includes metaphor, signification, symbolism, and communication.

Sender, Sol is a popular American graphic designer, best known for leading the design of the logo for Barack Obama's presidential campaign in 2008.

Senftenberg Egg, the was a student study by Peter Ghyczy in 1968. The VEB Synthesewerke Schwarzheide in Senftenberg in Eastern Germany started producing the garden chair, which reappeared in large numbers after the collapse of East Germany's Communist system.

Serif "Feet" or non-structural details at the ends of some strokes.

Set solid means to set lines of type without any vertical space between them.

Shakers, the were one of a few religious groups founded in the 18th century in England. Their dedication to handicraft paired with perfection, functionality and simplicity has resulted in a unique range of architecture and furniture that had a lasting influence on American design.

Sharp, Martin was an Australian artist and illustrator who is among others famous for his psychedelic posters of Bob Dylan and his classic "exploding" Jimi Hendrix poster, based on a photo by Linda McCartney.

Sherbow, Benjamin was an American copywriter who was employed for Calkins and Holden Advertising. It is said that Sherbow was the first person that worked as a typographer in a publicity firm in 1907. In 1922, Sherbow self-published "Effective Type-use for Advertising". This was six years before W. A. Dwiggins's "Layout in Advertising" and Tschichold's "Die Neue Typographie". The pioneering book focuses on rights and wrongs of typographic text and display.

Shirley Cards are colour reference cards that are used to perform skin-colour balance in still photography printing. A similar cinematic calibration technique is known as the China Girl.

hop

Shoulder.

Shoulder A curved stroke originating from a stem.
Skeleton black A black separation that adds detail and contrast only in the darkest section of the four-colour reproduction.

Rockwell

Rockwell, a slab serif face based on the geometric model.

Slab serif A slab serif, also called mechanistic, square serif, antique or Egyptian typeface is a typeface characterized by thick, block-like serifs that were invented during the nineteenth century in Britain. It was inspired by a new wave of advertising that needed bold type to catch the consumer's attention. In brief, they were designed to be noticed.
Small Caps Uppercase characters that appear as a smaller size than the capital height of a typeface. Short for "small capitals".

Smiley The smiley face as we know it today was made by Harvey Ross Ball, an American graphic artist. In 1963, Ball was employed by State Mutual Life Assurance Company of Worcester, Massachusetts (now known as Hanover Insurance Group) to create a happy face to raise the morale of the employees. Ball created the design in ten minutes and was paid $45.

Smiley 1963, Design: Harvey Ross Ball.

Snow White's Coffin The Braun SK4, known as "Snow White's Coffin" of 1956 is today frequently attributed solely to Dieter Rams. In fact, Hans Gugelot, the system designer at the Ulm School of Design (HfG Ulm), was a decisive influence upon the appearance of the combined phono-radio unit. The originally-shaped pick-up arm of this legendary unit, however, was designed by Wilhelm Wagenfeld for PC3, the precursor-model of the device, whose chassis the "Schneewittchensarg" adopted. In later the pick-up arm, whose shape did not accord well with the overall angular appearance of SK4, was replaced.

Braun SK4, 1956. Design: Dieter Rams, Hans Gugelot. © Braun.

Soft Sell is an advertisement that uses a non-aggressive sales message. The counterpart is a hard sell.

Spam mail The first spam mail was sent on May 3rd 1978 by Gary Thuerk. "I thought of it as e-marketing," he says about that first spam message, sent pre-Internet and two decades before most of the Americans were even getting their first email address.

Spanner, Russell was a Canadian furniture designer in the 50s. Less know is that he also was an amateur wrestling champion. He liked to test the strength and stability of his designs by jumping on them and throwing them across the factory floor.

Spiegel The only American designers ever featured on the cover of the German magazine were Raymond Loewy and Florence Knoll. The weekly news magazine was more focused on artist and architects: Thus in the 1950s and 1960s, Le Corbusier and Willi Baumeister appeared on the cover.

Spiekermann, Erik is not only known for his typefaces, he was a musician as well. To earn a bit on the side Spiekermann took on jobs as accompanying musician to such well-known German pop stars as Katja Ebstein.

Spine (Typography) The general curved stroke of a capital and lowercase S.

S

Spine of a lowercase or capital S.

Spine (Bookbinding) Backbone of a book. The spine is covered with the backstrip. In a book store, the details on the spine are what initially attract attention.

Get

Spur on the uppercase G.

Spur Slim projection from a curved stroke.

Stam, Mart was a popular Dutch furniture designer and architect. Less known is that his creation of a steel-tubing cantilever chair, using lengths of standard gas pipe and standard pipe joint fittings caused him serious trouble. In the late 1920s, Stam got involved in a patent lawsuit with Marcel Breuer. They both claimed to be the inventor of the basic cantilever chair design principle. Stam won the lawsuit but Breuer assigned the rights of his designs to Knoll, and for that reason it is possible to find the identical chair attributed to Stam in Europe and to Breuer in the United States.

Starbucks The world famous coffee company logo is actually depicting a siren. This symbol dates back to the old sailor tradition and of transporting coffee.

 STARBUCKS

Starbucks logo.

Starck, Philippe was the first designer to participate in the well-known TED Talks about Technology, Entertainment and Design.

Steinweiss, Alex "Smash Song Hits" by Rodgers & Hart is considered to be the first individually illustrated album cover art created by Alex Steinweiss in 1939. "The way records were sold was ridiculous," Mr. Steinweiss said in a 1990 interview. "The covers were brown, tan or green paper. They were not pleasing, and lacked sales appeal."

Stem A principally vertical letter stroke.

Stewardesses is the longest English expression you can type one-handed on a keyboard.

Stölzl, Gunta was a German textile artist and the Bauhaus's only female master in weaving. She applied ideas from modern art to weaving, experimented with synthetic materials and set up a dyeing facility. In 1925, when the Bauhaus moved from Weimar to Dessau, she became the school's first weaving director.

Stone, Sumner is a graphic artist and one of the first type designers to create his font family "Stone Serif, Sans and Informal" (1987) entirely at the computer.

Štorm, František is a Czech typographer who founded his own type foundry, Storm Type, in 1993. Outside the area of typography, Štorm is known as the vocalist/guitarist of the legendary black metal band Master's Hammer, established in 1987.

Gunta Stölzl's Bauhaus ID.

Straub, Marianne was one of the leading textile designers in Great Britain in the period from the 40s to 60s. She created upholstery for everything from BEA aircraft to London Underground.

Streamline Moderne is an Art Deco design and architecture style that emerged in the 1930s, especially in the US. Streamlining became a common design practice for cars, buses and even products like radios and toasters.

Streisand, Barbara The Streisand effect is the phenomenon whereby an attempt to censor or even remove a piece of information has the un-intended consequence of publicizing the information more widely, usually facilitated by the Internet. It is named after American entertainer Barbara Streisand, whose 2003 attempt to suppress photographs of her residence in Malibu, California, drew further public attention to it.

Strike, Lucky The brand's signature dark-green pack was changed to white in 1942. In a famous advertising campaign that used the slogan „Lucky Strike Green has gone to war", suggested by Raymond Loewy, the company claimed the change was made because the copper used in the green colour was needed for World War II. The white package actually was introduced to modernize the label and to increase the appeal of the package among female smokers. Market studies indicated that the green package was not appealing to women, who had become important consumers of tobacco products. The war effort became a convenient way to make the product more marketable while appearing patriotic at the same time.

Bocca, 1970. Design: Studio 65.
© www.ambientedirect.com

Stylorouge What first sounds like a lipstick brand, is a graphic design studio currently based in London. Formed by Rob O'Connor in 1981, Stylorouge since then was responsible for designing record sleeve designs for bands such as Crowded House, Simple Minds, Blur, Stereophonics and many more. The design studio was also responsible for the design of the original poster for the British film Trainspotting.

Subscript A subscript is a number, figure or symbol that is smaller than their normal line of type and appears at or slightly below the baseline. Subscripts are best known for their use in formulas and mathematical expressions.

Lucky Strike packaging, 1942.
© British American Tobacco.

Studio 65 The Designer group Studio 65 glorified Marilyn Monroe's lips. In 1970 they designed the sofa "Bocca" that immortalizes the shape of her lips.

Subtractive colour mixing.

Subtractive colour A term defining the three subtractive primary colours: cyan, magenta, and yellow. As opposed to the three additive colours: red, blue, and green.

Subvertising is the practice of altering product or political advertisements by disguising or parodying the original message to reveal new meanings and definitions, mainly to illustrate an antimessage.

Sullivan, Louis H. was an American architect (1856–1924) who was called the "father of skyscrapers" and "father of modernism". He is considered by many as the creator of the modern skyscraper, and was a mentor to Frank L. Wright, and an inspiration to the Chicago group of architects. Sullivan also coined the phrase "Form follows function" in 1896.

Sum The sum of all the numbers from one to hundred is 5050.

geometric or typographic designs. They are used over walls and sometimes floors and ceilings to create an illusion of expanded or altered space.

Supermarket principle In the US pavilion at Osaka for Expo 1970, Chermayeff and Geismar collected all the protective gloves and helmets that American workers wear and grouped similar objects to convey a collective idea. It was a means of calling attention to safety and to improved working conditions. The collection created an overall pattern that becomes something more than the sum of its parts.

Superscript is a number, figure or symbol that is smaller than their normal line of type and appears slightly above the baseline.

Quaderna, 1971. Design: Superstudio.
© Zanotta SpA – Italy.

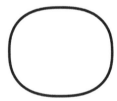

Superellipse.

Superellipse A superellipse is an oval shape which describes itself between a rectangle and a ellipse (or between a square and a circle). It is found in the layout principle of Donald E. Knuth's typeface Computer Modern and in Hermann Zapf's Melior Antiqua.

Supergraphics became the popular term in the late 60s for large-scale painted or applied decorative art in bold colours and typically in

Superstudio was an Italian architecture and design firm, founded in 1966 in Florence, Italy and part of the "anti-design" movement. One of their most famous pieces is "the Quaderna collection", which consists of a silk-screen printed grid.

Sutnar, Ladislav was a graphic designer from Czechoslovakia who was a pioneer of information design and information architecture. He is best known for his books: "Con-

Supergraphic Barangaroo Carpark Wayfinding, Lendlease. © THERE, Photography by Steve Brown.

trolled Visual Flow: Shape, Line and Colour", "Package Design: The Force of Visual Selling", and "Visual Design in Action: Principles, Purposes".

Swash Decorative letterform, usually applied for headings or as initial caps.

Swastika, the is an ancient religious symbol in Buddhism, Hinduism, and Jainism and dates back to the 2nd century BC. The name swastika comes from the Sanskrit word svastika, meaning "lucky or auspicious object". The symbol was adopted by the Nazi Party in 1920. In a lot of Western countries, the swastika has been removed or covered over because of its association with Nazism.

The swastika.

Swedish alphabet Before 2006, the rarely-used letter "W" in the Swedish alphabet wasn't a distinct letter, but a variant form of "V", pronounced identically. By 2006, "W" had become more popular in usage because of new loanwords, so it officially became a letter.

Swiss Punk This term identifies the Basle-based graphic designer Wolfgang Weingart. His poster designs caused a racket in the 1980s.

Symbol Sourcebook, the was published in 1972 by Henry Dreyfuss. It contains more than 20,000 symbols and is still considered a standard reference for all designers.

Syniuga, Siegfried Michail transformed a portrait of the sex goddess Brigitte Bardot into a chair. The chair was not being mass-produced and is considered a piece of art.

Syntax

Syntax Regular, 1968. Design: Hans Eduard Meier.

Syntax is a sans-serif font by Swiss designer Hans Eduard Meier, who had spent exactly 14 years working on the first ever "sans-serif Roman", from 1954 to 1968. Later on, the typeface was extended with additional serifs.

Szekely, Martin is a French product designer who became famous in the 1980s for his iconic Pi chair fabricated out of Carbon. In 1996 he suddenly made the decision to stop drawing: "It's the function of the objects ... that will now dictate their form", he explained.

Tail A descending stroke, often decorative.

Tail on uppercase R.

Talbot, William Fox was a British photography pioneer who is credited with the idea of halftone printing. In the early 1830s, he suggested using "photographic screens or veils" in connection with a photographic intaglio process.

Tale of Genji, the written by the female author Murasaki Shikibu in the early years of the 11th century is considered to be the world's first novel.

Tallon, Roger was a French industrial designer who started an enormous cult following with his design of a portable TV, called "Téléavia P111". The television was produced by the French firm Thomson SA. Its motto was "Téléavia, design also matters".

Tattoos were detested by famous architect Adolf Loos. In his text of 1908, Ornament and Crime it says: "A modern man who wears a tattoo is a criminal or degenerate. It is in prisons that 80 percent of inmates are found to have tattoos."

Teague, Walter Dorwin was an American industrial designer, architect and graphic designer. His book "Design This Day – The Technique of Order in the Machine Age", first published in 1940, was the first book to be written on the whole subject of industrial design.

TED (Technology, Entertainment, Design) is a global set of conferences run by the private non-profit Sapling Foundation, under the slogan "Ideas Worth Spreading". TED was founded in 1984 as a one-off event. TED's early emphasis was technology and design, consistent with its Silicon Valley origins, but it has since then broadened its focus to include talks on many scientific, cultural, and academic topics.

Stroke that lacks a serif.

Terminal The end of a stroke that lacks a serif.

The Face was a British music, culture and fashion magazine of the 1980s. From 1981 to 1986, Neville Brody was responsible as an art director for the magazine and established his use of experimental typographic design.

"The Who" logo, 1964. Design: Brian Pike.

The Who is one of the most influential rock groups of the 1960s and

1970s. Their famous "target" logo uses a custom font which was designed by the famous British artist Brian Pike in 1964 as a part of the original logo.

Thinking Man's Chair, 1988. Design: Jasper Morrison. © www.connox.de.

Thinking Man's Chair is one of the most famous creations by Jasper Morrison, originally developed as a prototype for a trade fair in Japan, the chair is not only an early work of the designer, but also an example for its moderate approach to design.

Bradbury Thompson's "Alphabet 26" font, 1958.

Thompson, Bradbury was a graphic designer of the twentieth century of American origin who developed a font called "Alphabet 26" or

"Monoalphabet". The font combined uppercase and lowercase forms of each letter to make the alphabet easier to learn and use.

Konsumstuhl Nr. 14, 1859. © Thonet GmbH, D-35066 Frankenberg. www.thonet.de.

Thonet, Michael was best known for his furniture and especially his chairs. Thonet's chair Nr. 14, also known as "Konsumstuhl Nr. 14" from 1859, is still called the "chair of chairs". The innovative wood bending technique allowed for the industrial production of a chair for the first time ever. Besides that the chair could be disassembled into a few components and therefore be exported to all nations of the world. The "Konsumstuhl" sold 50 million and is still in production.

MENINCHURNE
mountainous

Seven Line Grotesque, 1834. Design: William Thorowgood.

Thorowgood, William was a typographer, type founder and the first person to design a lowercase sans-serif typeface named "Seven Line Grotesque", released in 1834. This also meant the birth of the word "Grotesque".

Thumb index A thumb index, also called a cut-in index, is a series of round cut-outs in the pages of a book. Especially used for dictionaries or encyclopedias, to locate entries starting at a particular letter or section.

Thumbnail A thumbnail is a down-scaled-size version of the original image.

Thun, Matteo is an Italian designer and architect who defines his work as "eco – non ego".

TIFF stands for Tagged Image File Format and is a normally used file format for high colour depth pictures.

Tiffany & Co. logo on Tiffany Blue.

Tiffany Blue is the trademarked name for the light medium tone of robin egg blue associated with Tiffany & Co., the jewellery company. The custom Pantone number for PMS 1837, is based on the year the company was founded.

Time In most advertisements, the clocks are at 10:10. This should act friendlier as if they are at 4 o'clock The watches seem to smile.

Times New Roman The famed story of Times New Roman actually began as a challenge. In 1931, type designer Stanley Morison faulted London's newspaper "The Times" for being out of touch with modern typographical trends. So they asked him to create something better.

Times Roman The original hardware for the Times were created by the Monotype Corporation and the Linotype Company. Monotype labeled its type "Times New Roman," while Linotype named it "Times Roman." So nowadays when selecting "fonts" in your desktop publishing Apple users chose Linotype's font, while Microsoft users chose Monotype's.

Tironian notes.

Tironian notes are the shorthand signs of the ancient Romans, invented by Tiro (94 BC – 4 AD). His system consisted of about 4,000 abstract symbols and was extended to about 13,000 signs.

Title page The title page only contains the title in a fashion similar to the rest of the text within the book.

Tittle The dot on a lowercase i or j is called tittle or superscript dot.

Tofu is the nickname for the blank boxes that are shown when a computer or site lacks font support for a particular character.

Tittle on a lowercase i and j.

The "Registered Trademark" logo.

Tokyo In Tokyo, the inscription of the house numbers are assigned according to the order in which the building permits are issued.

Tomato is a design and film collective, founded in London in 1991. Less known is that the musicians Karl Hyde and Rick Smith of the electronic group Underworld are also part of Tomato.

Tombstone A hollow or filled rectangular or square character that is used to indicate the end of an article in a magazine.

Toscani, Oliveiro is an Italian photographer, who is best-known for his controversial advertising campaigns for Italian brand Benetton, from 1982 to 2000. One of his most famous pictures was the one of David Kirby dying of AIDS, surrounded by his grieving relatives. The image was first published in Life magazine, and later used for the United Colors of Benetton advertising campaign in 1992.

Total Design was the first design group established in The Netherlands. It was established by Wim Crouwel, Dick Schwarz, Friso Kramer, Paul Schwarz, and Benno Wissing in 1963. They were responsible for clients like the Stedelijk Museum and Randstad.

Tracking Amount of space that a type designer leaves between characters.

Trademark A trademark is usually a name, word, phrase, logo, symbol, design, image, or a combination of these elements used to identify and promote a product or service, and to protect it against any use by others.

The Bass Brewery's triangle became the first logo to be registered as a trademark in the UK, in 1876.

Trade Marks Registration Act In 1875 the Trade Marks Registration Act was sealed which allowed formal registration of trade marks in the UK for the first time.

Transliteration is the conversion of a text from one script to another, which is especially important for street signs, advertising or official documents.

Trojan Room coffee pot.

Trojan Room coffee pot The Trojan Room coffee pot was the inspiration for the world's first webcam. The coffee pot was located in the corridor just outside the so-called Trojan Room within the old Computer Laboratory of the University of Cambridge. It was made to help people working in other parts of the building avoid pointless trips to the coffee pot by providing, on the user's desktop computer, a live 128 × 128 greyscale picture of the state of the coffee pot.

Coral Light. Design: David Trubridge. © designlighting.com.

Trubridge, David is a furniture designer located in Whakatu, New Zealand. Trubridge's work has become widely recognized for its innovative, environmentally inspired qualities. Some of his collections are inspired by flora, fauna and formations within the landscape. His most known design is the iconic Coral Light, which is inspired by geometric polyhedron patterns of corals.

True Alphabet is a script that represents both vowels and consonants as letters equally. The first "true" alphabet was the Greek alphabet, which was developed on the basis of the earlier Phoenician alphabet.

The Penguin Composition Rules by Jan Tschichold.

Tschichold, Jan was a pioneer in typography and book design. Between 1947 – 1949, he lived in England where he redesigned up to 500 paperbacks published by Penguin Books. He introduced a standardized set of typographic rules, the Penguin Composition Rules. They include headings for various aspects of composition: Text Composition; Indenting of Paragraphs; Punctuation Marks and Spelling; Capitals, Small Capitals, and Italics; References and Footnotes; Folios; The Printing of Plays; The Printing of Poetry and Make-up.

Tufte, Edward Edward Rolf Tufte is noted for his writings on information design and as a pioneer in the field of data visualization. In 2010, President Barack Obama appointed Tufte to the American Recovery and Reinvestment Act's Recovery Independent Advisory Panel "to provide transparency in the use of Recovery-related funds."

Tuvalu Once known as the Ellice Islands, is a Polynesian island nation located in the Pacific Ocean. In 1998, Tuvalu began deriving revenue from the commercialisation of its ".tv" Internet domain name. The domain name generates about $2.2 million each year from royalties, which is about ten per cent of the government's total revenue.

Typecase A typecase is a compartmentalized wooden box. It is used to store movable type.

Typeface A typeface consists of a series of fonts and a full range of characters such as, numbers, letters, marks, and punctuation.

Type Foundry A company that designs or distributes typefaces. Companies that distribute digital typefaces are still referred to as foundries, even though no metal is cast.

Typography is the art and technique of arranging type to make written language legible, readable, and appealing when displayed. The arrangement of type involves selecting typefaces, point size, line length, line-spacing (leading), letter-spacing (tracking), and adjusting the space within letters pairs.

Type size The measure of a character's dimensions in points.

Type sizes

Excelsior	3 pt
Brilliant	4 pt
Pearl	5 pt
Nonpearl	6 pt
Minion	7 pt
Brevier	8 pt
Bourgeois	9 pt
Long Primer	10 pt
Small Pica	11 pt
Pica	12 pt
English	14 pt
Columbian	16 pt

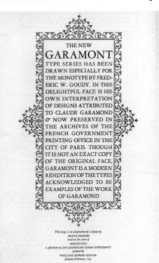

A specimen set by Bruce Rogers of Monotype's Garamont type in 1923.
© *James Puckett / Monotype*

Type specimen Printed document presenting a sample of the typefaces available from a foundry.

Twen Magazine was one of the most influential magazines. It was the groundbreaking design ideas, innovative usage of photography and full use of the advanced printing methods that made Twen a leader in magazine layout and design. Willy Fleckhaus was an art director of Twen from its beginnings in 1959 till its end in 1970. Fleckhaus was heavily influenced by the Swiss formalism shown in the layout of the Twen magazine.

He used rigid grid layout, simple typography and striking, often erotic, images. Fleckhaus used the 12 column grid in an interesting and innovative way because the format of the magazine was unusual large (265 × 335 mm).

Twen Magazine, 1959–1970.
© Twen Magazine.

Twombly, Carol is an American artist and typeface designer, who worked on typefaces, such as Trajan, Myriad and Adobe Caslon. Less known is that Twombly was the 1994 winner of the famous Prix Charles Peignot, given by the Association Typographique Internationale (ATypI). She was the first woman, and second American, to receive this award.

Masanori Umeda

Patricia Urquiola

Umeda, Masanori is a Japanese architect who is the creator of the iconic pop-museum-worthy "Tawaraya boxing ring bed" from 1981. The bed features a monochrome striped base with multicoloured "ropes" and light bulbs at each of the four corners of the ring and was made in collaboration with the famous Memphis group.

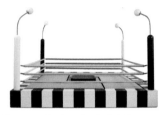

Tawaraya boxing ring bed, 1981. Design: Masanori Umeda.
© *www.memphis-milano.tumblr.com*

Uncial script is a script written entirely in capital letters commonly used from the 4th to 8th centuries AD by Latin and Greek scribes. The letter-shapes are rounded with fewer strokes, and the text was written with no spaces between words to increase writing speed. The Book of Kells, for example, is lettered in a variety of uncial script that originated in Ireland.

uncial

Uncial script.

Uncoated Paper is a paper that doesn't have a coating applied to it for smoothness.

Unicode is an international standard for encoding text. It was invented in 1992 and contains more than 128,000 characters, including 135 modern and historic scripts, as well as multiple symbol sets.

Unigrid System, 1977. Design: Massimo Vignelli. © *US National Park Service.*

Unigrid System One of the most successful projects of the Federal Design Improvement program was the Unigrid System, developed by Massimo Vignelli, Vincent Gleason, and Dennis McLaughlin in 1977 for the US National Park Service. The Unigrid unified the hundreds of informational folders used at about 350 different locations. The standardized format allowed the NPS to created brochures in ten basic formats and to keep a consistent, recognizable structure across all its materials.

Unity symbol The unity symbol represents the two symbols Mars (meaning masculinity or War God) and Venus (meaning femininity or Dear Goddess), which was first used in about 450 BC, according to Greek mythology. Even today this image is still used and shows the link between man and woman. The symbol of unity demonstrates love, confidence, loyalty and solidarity.

![Univers font family display]

Univers font family, 1954. Design: Adrian Frutiger.

Univers is a sans-serif typeface designed by Adrian Frutiger in 1954. For the first time Univers treated a font family as a complete, cohesive system for the first time. Starting point is the regular font (Univers 55), from which all others are derived. In the Netherlands, Univers became an unofficial national font, while designers in Germany and the USA favoured Helvetica.

Universale was the first chair entirely made out of plastic by the injection-moulding technique. It was designed by Joe Colombo in 1965.

Unknown Pleasures is the debut studio album (1979) by the English rock band Joy Division. The record cover was designed by Peter Saville who choose an image of radio waves from pulsar CP 1919, from The Cambridge Encyclopaedia of Astronomy. The image was initially created by radio astronomer Harold Craft. Susie Goldring, reviewing the album for BBC Online said, " ... its white on black lines reflect a pulse of power, a surge of bass, and raw angst. If the cover doesn't draw you in, the music will."

Upper and lower case was one of the first publications intended specifically for the design community, in 1973. U&lc was a product of American graphic designer Herbert F. (Herb) Lubalin and the International Typeface Corporation with the aim to display and advertise the latest typefaces from ITC.

U&lc was a product of Herb Lubalin and the International Typeface Corporation.

Uppercase A letter or group of letters of the size and form generally used to begin sentences and proper nouns. Also known as "capital letters".

Urquiola, Patricia is a Spanish architect and designer whose work is characterized by handicraft. Less known is that she was mentored by some of the masters of Italian industrial design. Achille Castiglioni for example oversaw her graduate thesis.

Vacat Page An intentionally blank page or vacat page is a page that is devoid of content. Such pages may serve from place-holding to space-filling and content separation. Vacat Pages are usually the result of printing conventions and techniques.

Vaio logo. Design: Tomothy © Sony Corporation.

Vaio standing for Visual Audio Intelligent Organizer, is a manufacturer of personal computers and was originally a brand of Sony Corporation. The logo concept was created by Teiyu Goto while it was designed by Timothy Hanley. The wordmark shows a stylized letter combination of "VA" to look like a sine wave and "IO" to refer to binary digits 1 and 0. It should reflect the merging of analog and digital signals.

Vantablack is the blackest black known, absorbing up to 99.96 % of radiation in the visible spectrum.

Vaporware A term that is generally used to describe a hardware or software product that has been announced, but is never actually manufactured nor cancelled.

Varnish A liquid coating applied to a surface for protection and for a glossy effect.

Vector Graphic Vector graphics allow the designer to expand or reduce a graphic in size without any loss in quality using curves, points, lines, and polygons.

The Ramones Logo, 1975. Design: Arturo Vega.

Vega, Arturo was the creative director of the 1970s punk band The Ramones. Just as the band's sound inspired generations, so did the band's logo, which used the seal of the President of the United States as a starting point. Vega explained: "I saw them as the ultimate all-American band. To me, they reflected the American character in general an almost childish aggression."

Steve Jobs' 256-foot yacht Venus. © charterworld.com.

Venus is a super yacht designed by Philippe Starck's design company Ubik for Steve Jobs. However, Jobs died in October 2011, the yacht was

Ver Sacrum

unveiled a year later for more than 90 million Dollar.

Ver Sacrum was an experimental design magazine of the Vienna Secession, released from 1898–1903. Ver Sacrum means "Sacred Spring" in Latin.

Verso The left-hand page of a book or a manuscript.

Ver Sacrum magazine.

Vetter, Hans Adolf was an Austrian-American architect. Vetter not only created buildings, he also wrote poems on steel-tube furniture. Here an excerpt: "Swaying on its bending carriage/on a carpet, on the parquet/Cut into a set of spirals/rearing up the riddled board. In the empty tubes there flowing/streaming from a sourceless well/Outer splendor, inner darkness, Lines perpetually parallel. So that one apply to many / Model will embrace them all/Touch, and you feel the coldness Look, and you will spot the norm: /Put to life in sinuous subjection, an existence, soulless form."

Victore, James is an American art director, designer, and author. He is also the initiator of "The Dinner Series", which is a 4-day workshop that includes dinner and discussion with leading figures in the arts, creativity and culture.

The famous typographic V&A Logo, 1990. Design: Alan Fletcher.

Victoria and Albert Museum, the is the world's largest museum of decorative arts and design. Situated in London, the Victoria and Albert Museum, often abbreviated as the V&A, houses over 4.5 million objects.

View from the Window at Le Gras, Nicéphore Niépce, 1826–27.

View from the Window at Le Gras is the oldest surviving camera photograph. It was created by Nicéphore Niépce in 1826 or 1827 at Saint-Loup-de-Varennes in France. It shows parts of the buildings and surrounding countryside of his estate, Le Gras, as seen from a high window.

164

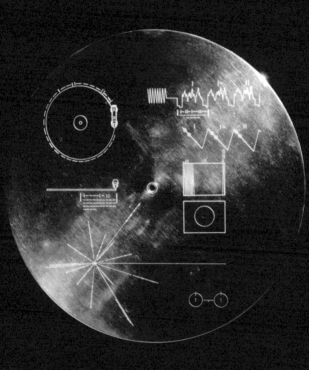

Voyager Golden Record. 1977.

Massimo Vignelli in his office in New York.

on both Voyager spacecraft. They contained sounds and images selected to portray the diversity of life and culture on Earth, and are intended for any intelligent extra-terrestrial life form, or for future humans, who may find them.

Vignelli, Massimo was one of the most versatile designers who is best known for his design for the New York City Subway map. He was not only a devoted graphic designer of public signage but also designed corporate identities, products and furniture. His ethos was, "If you can design one thing, you can design everything".

Visorium A small wooden stand on which the typesetter puts the typescript he is typesetting.

Vogue The famous fashion magazine published its very first colour photo cover in July, 1932. It was art directed by Mehemed Fehmy Agha. He was a Russian-born Turkish designer, art director, and pioneer of modern American publishing.

Vocabulary It is a common notion that the average English-speaking adult knows between 20,000 and 30,000 words.

Voormann, Klaus is a German musician, artist and record producer. His most notable work as a designer is the cover for the album Revolver by the Beatles in 1966. For this work, he won the Grammy Award for Best Album Cover.

Voyager Golden Record, the is a phonograph record that was placed

W

W Various computer keyboards in the White House are missing the key "W" which is President Bush's middle initial. In some cases the "W" is marked out, but the most prevalent example is the key being removed. They finally accused the Clinton staff of vandalising the inventory of the White House and removing the missing keys.

Bronze cast of "This is a printing office" by Beatrice Warde, 1932.

Waldi The Dachshund-shaped figure advertised the Olympic Games in Munich in 1972. It was designed by Otl Aicher.

Walker is the name of a sans-serif typeface made by Matthew Carter for the Walker Arts Center. It is the first typeface that has up to 5 modular "snap-on" serifs that can be attached to each letterform using keystroke commands.

Wanders, Marcel is a Dutch designer and co-founder of the successful design label Moooi. He became internationally known by his iconic Knotted Chair, which combines industrial techniques and handcrafting. The New York Times described him as the Lady Gaga of the design world. Less known is that his out-of-the-box thinking got him expelled from the Design Academy in Eindhoven.

Knotted Chair, Droog, 1995. Design: Marcel Wanders. © connox.

Warde, Beatrice Born on September 20th, 1900 Warde was one of the first female typographers. Her "This is a Printing Office" broadside, designed to showcase Gill's Perpetua titling capitals, was published in 1932. It was one of many broadsides Monotype produced, to display their typefaces. A bronze cast of the broadside is mounted at the entrance to the US Government Publishing Office.

Washi is a special paper made in Japan. The notion comes from wa "Japanese" and shi "paper". Washi is used to describe paper made by hand in the traditional manner.

Watermark Translucent picture impressed on paper created during manufacture. A watermark becomes visible when held to light.

Watts, Charlie The drummer of the Rolling Stones is actually a trained professional designer, who worked for an advertising agency based in

London. Watts wrote and illustrated a book on jazz legend Charlie Parker, which bears the title: "Ode to a High Flying Bird".

Kem Weber's "Airline Chair", 1934.

Weber, Kem was a furniture and industrial designer who designed several iconic "Streamline" objects, that emphasized curving forms and long horizontal lines. His most famous work is probably the "Airline" chair of 1934.

Website The first ever website in the world was info.cern.ch.

Wedgwood, Thomas is most widely known as the first person to have attempted to photograph the image formed in a camera obscura, around 1800.

Wegner, Hans Jørgensen was a Danish furniture designer who designed over 500 different chairs. A lot of them have become recognizable design icons, like the "Peacock chair" or the "Wishbone chair".

Weidemann, Kurt was one of the most influential German designer and typographer. Weidemann also worked as an consultant to compa-

nies. Funny is that Weidemann's note paper depicts himself as a fool advising a king. The illustration was made by an artist friend of his, Jan Peter Tripp.

The king and his fool. © Jan Peter Tripp.

Weight Refers to the thickness of a letter. Letters with the thinnest weight variants are called Ultralight, Light and Thin, while the thickest are referred to as Bold, Ultra Bold, Extra Bold, Black, Ultra Black and Extra Black.

"Wishbone chair", 1949. Design: Hans J. Wegner. © designice.com.

Weil, Daniel is an Argentinian architect and industrial designer who has been working for Knoll, Alessi, and Swatch and has been a partner of Pentagram in London. His iconic

Radio Bag, 1983. Design: Daniel Weil. © Daniel Weil.

work also includes the "Radio Bag" from 1982, a radio taken apart and put into a transparent bag, which perfectly met the anarchic punk aesthetic at that time.

Well, Darius In 1827 Darius Well invented the lateral router for mass producing of woodtype letters. The router could cut curved outlines in wood.

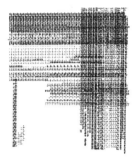

A "typestract" by H.N. Werkman, 1923 – 9.

Werkman, Hendrik Nicolaas was an experimental Dutch artist, typographer and printer. In May 1940, soon after the German invasion of the Netherlands, Werkman started a clandestine publishing house, called De Blauwe Schuit ("The Blue Barge"), which ran to forty publications.

Logo of the NBA.

West, Jerry is a retired American basketball player who is nicknamed

"The Logo" in reference to his silhouette being pictured in the NBA logo.

ABCDEFGHIJKLM

Westminster, 1965. Design: Leo Maggs.

Westminster is a typeface inspired by the machine-readable numbers printed on cheques, like E-13B. It was designed by Leo Maggs in the 1965.

White space The area where there is no text or graphics. Essentially, the negative space of the page design that needs to be designed as well.

Widow A paragraph-ending line that falls at the beginning of the following page or column, thus separated from the rest of the text.

Width Refers to the width of a character. Width can range from extended to condensed, in reference to the standard weight of the character, known as regular or normal.

Wilanów Poster Museum, the is the world's oldest poster museum. It was founded 1968 near Warsaw, Poland at the Wilanów Palace complex. More than 55,000 posters are in the actual collection.

Wilder, Billy The famous filmmaker was friends with Charles and Ray Eames. They even accompanied Billy and Audrey Wilder on their honeymoon in June and July 1948.

Wilp, Charles Paul was a German advertising-designer, artist, photographer and short-movie-editor. Wilp developed a few of the most important advertisements of the 1960s and 70s: Puschkin ("Wodka for real men", 1963), Pirelli and Volkswagen (VW-Käfer-Slogan: "It runs ... and runs ... and runs"). He was also an image consultant for major politicians, such as Willy Brandt.

Wilson, Robert In 2003, Wilson produced the musical "The White Town" at the Bellevue Theatre in Klampenborg, in the north of Copenhagen. The show focuses on Arne Jacobsen, who designed the theatre.

Windsor is a serif typeface which is used in almost all title sequences and credits of Woody Allen's films, beginning with 1977's Annie Hall. Allen preferred to use the sparse white Windsor Light Condensed over a black background. Windsor was created by Eleisha Pechey in 1905.

Movie Title Screen for Woody Allen's Annie Hall, set in Windsor Light Condensed. Design: Eleisha Pechey.

Wittgenstein, Ludwig When Otl Aicher was commissioned to create a Corporate Design for Franz Schneider Brakel (FSB) he began to look around for a door-handle shape that was as simple as it was symbolic. He found the appropriate model in the mountain of a door that the philosopher Ludwig Wittgenstein had created in the course of designing – from 1926 to 1928 – a house for his sister.

Wittkugel, Klaus was one of the most important commercial poster artists in the German Democratic Republic. It was he who in the second half of the 1950s "ringed" the Lufthansa crane and not, as is so often assumed Otl Aicher.

Wobo The idea of turning waste into useful products came to life in 1963 with the Heineken Wobo (World Bottle). Envisioned by beer brewer Alfred Heineken and designed by Dutch architect John Habraken, the "brick that holds beer" was ahead of its ecodesign time. Heineken's idea came after travelling to the Caribbean where he saw two problems: beaches littered with bottles and a lack of affordable building materials. The Wobo became his vision to solve both the recycling and housing challenges that he had witnessed on the islands. Today, a shed at the Heineken estate and a wall made of Wobo at the Heineken Museum in Amsterdam are the only structures where the "beer brick" was used.

Wolfe, Tom Author of the famous bestseller "Bonfire of the Vanities" made fun of the Bauhaus staff in his book "From Bauhaus to our House", which came out in 1981.

Wonderground Map, the was a London Underground map designed in 1914 by MacDonald Gill, the younger brother of type designer Eric Gill. The mainly coloured Wonderground map was a mixture of cartoon, fantasy, and topological accuracy and became an instant hit. It is known today as the map which saved the London underground by encouraging off-peak travel.

Wonderground Map (detail), 1914.
Design: MacDonald Gill.

Woodcut is a relief printing technique from planks of incised wood.
It is one of the oldest methods of
making prints from a relief surface. They used to print on textiles
in China since the 5th century AD.

Word frequency The ten most
common words in English:

1	the
2	be
3	to
4	of
5	and
6	a
7	in
8	that
9	have
10	I

Word of the Year Since 1991, the
American Dialect Society (ADS)
has designated one or more words
or terms to be the "Word of the
Year" in the United States. In
1990 the first Word of the Year was
"bushlips" originated from President George H. W. Bush's 1988
"Read my lips: no new taxes" bro-
ken promise.

World Design Capital The World
Design Capital (WDC) is a city
promotion project by the International Council of Societies of Industrial Design (ICSID), founded in
1957. The aim of the organization
is to award accomplishments made
by cities around the world in the
field of design. World Design Capitals by year: Torino, Italy (2008),
Seoul, South Korea (2010), Helsinki, Finland (2012), Cape Town,
South Africa (2014), Taipei, Taiwan (2016), Mexico City, Mexico
(2018).

Worm A worm (Abbreviation for
Write Once, Read Many) is an optical disc that can only be imaged
once and the data can't be erased.

Wove paper Paper with a very uniform surface and no ribbing, similar in appearance to parchment.
Its flat surface allowed for finer
printing of texts and engravings.

Wright, Frank Lloyd In Wright's
architectural office in Taliesin,
Wisconsin the flies were alter-
nately called Gropius or Corbu.
You may ask why? Because Wright
wasn't a big admirer of the work of
Le Corbusier and Walter Gropius.

Wyman, Lance is an American
graphic designer and a pioneer in
logo design. He is probably best
known for his visual identity of
the 1968 Summer Olympic Games
in Mexico, following work with
designing graphic programs for
the Mexico City Metro and the
1970 World Cup competition.

WYSIWYG The term "What You
See Is What You Get" should reflect the approx. screen representation of what the final printed
image will look like.

X
Y
Z

x-height The height of the main body of a lowercase letter.

Xylography A relief printing technique, also called block printing or woodcut.

"Butterfly Stool", 1954. Design: Sori Yanagi. www.ambientedirect.com.

Yanagi, Sori was a Japanese product designer who is most famous for his iconic Butterfly Stool. His products illustrate his thinking: "True beauty is not made, it is born naturally".

Yellow One of the four-colour process inks, made from the organic pigment diarylide yellow, formerly called benzidine yellow.

Yellowing Process of discolouration of white paper due to aging.

Yes Men, the are a culture jamming activist duo composed of Jacques Servin and Igor Vamos. They gained worldwide notoriety for impersonating the World Trade Organization on television and at business conferences around the world.

Yo is a social media application Its only function was to send the user's friends the word "yo".

Yokoo, Tadanori is a Japanese designer and visual artist. Because his work was so inspired by 1960s pop culture, he has often been described as the "Japanese Andy Warhol".

Yoshioka, Tokujin is a Japanese artist and designer who is responsible for the world biggest optical glass table named "Waterfall". It is a 4.5 meter giant optical glass block which reminds of water running down the surface of a cliff.

Zanuso, Marco was an Italian architect and designer who was supporting the idea of "good design" in the postwar years. In 1957 he partnered with Richard Sapper and they quickly became pioneers in applying new shapes and materials.

Hermann Zapf's drawing for Optima on a 1000-lira bill © Monotype.

Zapf, Hermann Once made a trip to the Franciscan church of Santa Croce in Florence in 1950. Zapf screened the 276 gravestones in a different light than the other tourists. He was fascinated by the typeface diversity set in stone. Because he has forgotten his sketchbook at the hotel, Zapf had to draw some of the letters for his future Optima typeface on a 1000-lira bill.

Zaum was an expression invented by Russian Futurists in 1912 to demonstrate that a word can be given

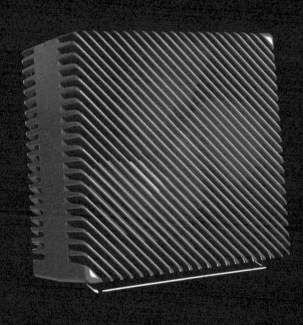

Marco Zanuso's "Ariante" fan for Vortice. © Design Photographs Austin Calhoon.

any meaning. Zaum, they claimed, wasn't meant to mean anything at all.

Zündapp Janus is a car model made in Germany between 1957 and 1958. The only car ever made by the company was named Zündapp Janus, a four-seater car, where the two front and two rear passengers sat back to back, to optimally use the enclosed space.

Zündapp Janus 250. © Wikipedia.

Zwart, Piet was a Dutch photographer, typographer, and industrial designer, who was awarded with the "Designer of the Century" award by the Association of Dutch Designers in 2000.

Zyzzyva is the last word in most of the English-language dictionaries. It is a genus of tropical American weevil often destructive to plants.

INDEX

A

A 6
Aalto Vase, the 6
Aardvark 6
Aarnio, Eerio 6
Abrogans 6
Accolade 6
Accordion fold 6
Acrobat 6
Acronym 6
Acrostic 6
Action office, the 6
Adbusters 8
Additive colour 8
Adenauer, Konrad 8
Adidas 8
Adobe 8
Adorno, Theordor W. 8
Adshel 8
Advertorial 8
AEG 8
Affair of the Placards, the 9
Affiche 9
Agate 9
Agha, Mehemed Fehmy 9
Aicher, Otl 9
AIGA 9
Albers, Anni 9
Albers, Josef 10
Albus, Volker 10
Aldine Press 10
Aldus leaf 10
Aldus Manutius 10
Aleph 11
Alignment 11
Alpha channel, the 11
Alphanumeric 11
American Quarto 11
Ampersand 11
Amplitude 11
Amplitude modulation 11
Analog Proof 11
Anchor Point 11
Anglepoise lamp 11
Animated GIF 12

Anna G 12
ANSI 12
Anti-aliasing 12
Anti-Design 12
Antiqua 12
Antique 12
Antique Olive 12
Aperture 14
Apex 14
Appendix 14
Apple Macintosh 14
Arad, Ron 14
Architecture 14
Architype Van Doesburg 14
Arm 14
Arntz, Gerd 14
Art Director 15
Arts & Architecture 15
Arts & Crafts movement, the 15
Ascender 15
ASCII 15
Asterisk 15
Asymmetrical 15
At sign 15
Auerbach, Johannes Ilmari 15
Authagraph 17
Avant Garde 17
Averill, Steve 17

B

B42 19
Baas, Maarten 19
Babel Fish 19
Backslant 19
Backslash 19
Bad Break 19
Balla, Giacomo 19
Ballpoint pen 19
Ball terminal 19
Bang 19
Banham, Stephen 21
Bantjes, Marian 21
Bar 21
Barcelona chair, the 21

Barcode 21
Barnack, Oskar 21
Barnbrook, Jonathan 21
Baseline 22
Baseline Magazine 22
Baskerville, John 22
Bass, Saul 22
Bastard type 22
Bayer, Herbert 22
Beall, Lester 23
Beck, Henry Charles 23
Behrens, Peter 23
Bel Geddes, Norman 23
Bell Centennial 23
Bellini, Carlo 23
Benguiat, Ed 24
Bennett, Ward 24
Bensistor, the 24
Bentley 24
Benton, Morris Fuller 24
Berliner 24
Berners-Lee, Tim 24
Bernhard, Lucian 24
Bertoia, Harry 24
Bevel 24
Bézier Curve 24
Biáng 24
Bible 25
Bild 25
Billboard 25
Bill, Max 25
Biomorphism 25
Bi Sheng 25
Bit 25
Bitmap 26
Bitstream Inc. 26
Black Flag 26
Blackletter 26
Blackspot Sneaker, the 26
Blase, Karl-Oskar 26
Bleed 28
Bley, Thomas S. 28
Blind de/embossing 28
Blind folio 28
Block quotation 28
Blow 28

Blueline 28
Bluffalo Bill 28
Blur 28
Blurb 28
BMW Culture Book, the 28
Boards 29
Bodoni, Giambattista 29
Body type 29
Bofinger chair, the 29
Book formats 29
Book of Kells 29
Boom, Irma 29
Border 30
Bormann Decree, the 30
Boros, Christian 30
Bouma 30
Bowl 30
BP 30
Bracket 30
Braille, Louis 30
Branding 31
Brandt, Marianne 31
Broadsheet 31
Brodovitch, Alexey 31
Brody, Neville 31
Brownjohn, Robert 31
Buckyballs 31
Bullet 31
Bulls Eye 31
Burrill, Anthony 32
Burri, René 31
Buzzword 32
BYGMCR 32
Byline 32
Byrne, David 32

C

Calka, Maurice 34
Calkins, Ernest Elmo 34
Camel 34
Cantilever chair, the 34
Capote, Truman 34
Care Package 34
Carson, David 34

Index

Casino 34
Caslon, William 34
Cassandre, A.M. 34
Caxton, William 35
CBS 35
CC 35
CD-ROM 35
Century Guild, The 35
Chair Thing, the 35
Chaise Longue LC4 35
Chalet 35
Chanel 36
Chicago 36
Chinese 36
Chip Kidd 36
Christian Schwartz 36
Chroma 36
Chruxin, Christian 36
Chupa Chups 36
Chwast, Seymour 37
Cicero 37
Circumflex 37
Clarendon 37
Clip art 37
CMYK 37
Coated Paper 37
Coca-Cola 37
Codex 37
Coffins 38
Coiner, Charles Toucey 38
Colani 38
Colani GT 38
Collins, Brian 38
Collotype 38
Colombo, Joe 38
Colophon 38
Colour Blindness 38
Compasso d'Oro 38
Complementary Colours 39
Composing stick 39
Condensed Type 39
Cooper Oswald B. 39
Cooper Union 39
Cornelius 39
Counter 40
Courier 40

Cranbrook Academy of Art, the 40
Crasset, Matali 40
Crossbar 40
Crouwel, Wim 40
Culture Jamming 40
Cursive 40
Curtis, David Hillman 40
Cuts 41
Cut-up technique 41
Cyan 41
Cyberspace 41

D

Dagger 43
Danziger, Louis 43
Dauphine 43
Dazzle camouflage 43
De Bono, Edward 43
Declaration of Independence 43
Decorative line 43
Denotation 44
Descender 44
Design Award 44
Designers Republic, the 44
Design for the real world 44
Design Museum, the 44
Design Revue 44
De Stijl 44
Devanagari 45
De Vinne, Theodore Low 45
Diacritic 45
Diagonal Stroke 45
Diamond Sutra 45
Dictionary 45
Didone 46
Didot, Firmin 46
Didot, François-Ambroise 46
Die Cut 46
Diffrient, Niels 46
Digi Grotesk 46
Digiset 46
Digital 46
Digraph 46
Diminuendo 46

DIN 1451 46
Dingbat 47
Diphthong 47
Dogcow 47
Dog Ear 47
Dog Lamp 47
Domains 47
Dot Dot Dot 49
Dot Gain 49
DOT pictograms, the 49
Double Page Spread 49
Double-Truck 49
Doyle, Christopher 49
DPI 49
Dresser, Christopher 49
Dreyfuss, Henry 49
Drop Shadow 49
Dummy 50
Duotone 50
Dutch Alphabet 50
Dwiggins, William Addison 50
Dylan, Bob 50
Dymaxion car, the 50

E

E-13B 52
Eames Lounge Chair 52
Eames, Ray 52
Ear 52
Edelmann, Heinz 52
Edition Suhrkamp 52
Ehrlich, Franz 52
Elements of Euclid, the 53
E-Mail 53
Embedding 53
Emboss 53
Emigre 53
Emoticon 53
Em space 53
Engelbart, Douglas 53
English Finish 53
Engraving 53
En space 53
Ephemera 53

EPS 53
Ericofon, the 54
Ernst, Jupp 54
Error 404 54
Esquire 54
Esslinger, Hartmut 54
Estienne, Robert 54
Eszett 54
Etaoin shrdlu 54
Etch 55
Eternity 55
Euro currency sign 55
Eurostile 55
Exclamation mark 56
Exlibris 56
Experimental Jetset 56
Expert font 56
Extenders 56
Eye 56

F

Facsimile 58
Fagen, Donald 58
Fairey, Shepard 58
False Friend 58
Family of Man, the 58
Fat Faces 58
Faux bold 58
Features of Letters 58
Federalist flag, the 58
FedEx 58
Fehlbaum, Rolf 59
Feliciano, Felice 59
Fella, Ed 59
Fetter, William 59
Finial 59
Fischer, Volker 59
Fisher Price 60
Flag of the United States 60
Fleckhaus, Willy 60
Flexography 60
Flusser, Villém 60
Focal Point 60
Font 60

Index

Form follows function 60
Fornasetti, Piero 60
Forty 60
Four-colour process, the 60
Fournier, Pierre-Simon 62
Fraktur 62
Frankfurt Kitchen 62
Franklin Gothic 62
Frankl, Paul Theodore 62
Fregio Megano 63
Frequency modulation 63
Fridolin 63
Frigidaire 63
Frisch, Max 63
Frontispiece 63
Fukuda, Shigeo 64
Fuller, Richard Buckminster 64
Futhark 64
Futura 64
Futurist Manifesto 64

G

Games, Abram 66
Gap 66
Garamond, Claude 66
Garfunkel, Art 66
Garland, Ken 66
Garrett, Malcolm 66
Gastrotypographicalassemblage 67
Gatefold 67
Gaul, Albro T. 67
Gautschen 67
Gehry, Frank 67
Gentleman's Magazine, the 67
German Dictionary, the 67
Gerstner, Karl 67
Gesamtkunstwerk 67
Ghosting 68
Gibson, William 67
GIF 68
Ginzburg, Ralph 68
Girard, Alexander 68
Gismondi, Ernesto 68

Giugiaro, Giorgetto 68
Glaser, Milton 68
Global Tools 68
Gloor, Beat 69
Glyph 69
Goertz, Albrecht von 69
Goethe, Johann W. von 69
Goldfish 69
Gomringer, Eugen 69
Good Design 69
Google 69
Gotham 69
Graham, John J. 70
Graphem 70
Graves, Michael 70
Gray, Eileen 70
Greeking 70
Griffo, Francesco 70
Grillo 70
Gropius, Walter 72
Groundwood 72
Guardian, the 72
Guerrilla marketing 72
Gugelot Design 72
GUI 72
Guillemets 72
Guixé, Martí 72
Gutter 72

H

Häberli, Alfredo 74
Haeckel, Ernst 74
Haiku 74
Hairline 74
Half title 74
Halftone 74
Halloween, Örni 74
Hamilton, Richard 74
Han characters 74
Harrison, Christopher Guy 74
Hawaii 74
Heartfield, John 76
Heizölrückstoßabdämpfung 76
Helvetica 76

Henrion, Frederick Henri Kay 76
Hergé 77
Hexachrome 77
Hickey 77
Highway Gothic 77
Hilton, James 77
Hipgnosis 77
Hirche, Herbert 78
HKS 78
Hobo Signs 78
Hoffmann, Josef 78
Hofmann, Armin 78
Horgan, Stephen H. 79
Horntrich, Günter 79
Hot Spot 79
House Sheet 79
How High the Moon 79
HTML 79
HTTP 79
Hunt, Robert 79
Huszár, Vilmos 79
Hypertext 79
Hyphen 79

I

IBM 82
Iceland 82
Ideograph 82
Igarashi, Takenobu 82
Ikarus 82
IKEA 82
Imposition 82
Imprimatur 82
Incipit 82
Incunable 82
Initial 82
Ink set-off 82
Ink Trap 83
Insertio 83
Interleaves 83
International Symbol of Access 83
International Typeface Corporation, the 83
Interrobang 83

Interstate 83
Iribe, Paul 83
ISO 7001 83
Isogram 83
Isotype 84
Italic 84
Itten, Johannes 84
IX monogram, the 84

J

J 86
Jacket 86
Jackson, Dakota 86
Jacobsen, Arne 86
Jandl, Ernst 86
Janoff, Rob 86
Japanese E-Mail 87
Jenson, Nicholas 87
Johnston, Edward 87
Jones, Allen 87
Jongerius, Hella 87
Joop, Wolfgang 87
Jordan, Paul 87
Journeyman printer 87
JPEG 88
Juhl, Finn 88

K

Kalman, Tibor 90
Kamekura, Yasuka 90
Kare, Susan 90
Kauffer, Edward McKnight 90
Keeler, Christine 90
Kepes, György 90
Kerning 90
Kern, the 90
Key Plate 91
Kicker 91
Kiesler, Frederick John 91
Kiss Impression 91
Klint, Kaare 91
Koch, Rudolf 91

Index

Kraft Paper 91
Kramer, Ferdinand 92
Kruger, Barbara 92
Kühn, Heinrich 92
Kukkapuro, Yrjö 92
Kupetz, Günter 92

Lufthansa 100
Lustig, Alvin 100
Luthe, Claus 100
Lutz, Rudolph 101
Lynch, David 101

L

Lacoste 94
Lagerfeld, Karl 94
Lambie-Nairn, Martin 94
László, Paul 94
Latin Alphabet, the 94
Lazarus, Emma 94
Leading 95
Le Corbusier 95
Lengyel, Stefan 95
Lenna 95
Lepoix, Louis L. 95
Leporello 95
Less is more 96
Letraset 96
Letter Gothic 96
Letterpress 96
Leupin, Herbert 96
Levi's 501 96
Ligature 96
Link 96
Linotype machine, the 97
Lipogram 97
Lissitzky, Lazar Markovich 97
Loesch, Uwe 97
Loewy, Raymond 97
Logo 97
Longest English Sentence 98
Longplayer 98
Loop 98
Loos, Adolf 98
Lord Kitchener Wants You 98
Lorem ipsum 98
Lorenz Static, the 98
Lovegrove, Ross 100
Lowercase 100
Lucida 100

M

Mackmurdo, Arthur Heygate 103
Madison Avenue 103
Magazine 103
Magenta 103
Malevich, Kazimir 103
Maloof, Sam 103
Manuale Typografico 103
Mari, Enzo 103
Mariscal, Javier 104
Mason 104
Masthead 104
Matrix 104
Matter, Herbert 104
MAYA 104
McElroy, Neil Hosler 104
Mead, Syd 105
Meggs, Philip Baxter 105
Mellor, David 105
Memphis Group 105
Mendini, Alessandro 105
Mergenthaler, Ottmar 105
Meta 106
Metamerism 106
Michelin 106
Milk 106
Miller, Herman 106
Mistral 108
Mnemonic 108
Mock Up 108
Modulor, the 108
Moholy-Nagy, László 108
Moiré 108
Mollino, Carlo 108
Monarch 108
Monogram 108
Monospaced Font 109
Monotype 109

Mont Blanc 109
Morrison, Jasper 109
Moss, Kate 109
Mourgue, Oliver 109
Mrs Eaves 109
Mr. Yuk 109
MTV 110
Muji 110
Mukai, Shutaro 110
Multiple master fonts 110
Munari, Bruno 111
Munsell colour system, the 111
Museum of Modern Art 111
Muthesius, Eckart 111
Muybridge, Eadward 111
M Weight, the 111
Myriad 111

N

NASA 113
National Medal of Arts 113
Negative Space 113
Nelson, George 113
Neruda, Pablo 113
Neurath, Otto 113
Neutraface 113
New Bauhaus, the 115
Newson, Marc 115
Newspaper 115
Newspaper format 115
NeXT 115
Nike 115
Nixon, Richard 115
Noguchi, Isamu 115
No Logo 116
Noto 116
N. W. Ayer & Son 116

O

Oblique 118
OCR-A 118
OCR-B 118

Octavo 118
Ogilvy, David 118
OK 118
OK sheet 118
Old German paper sizes 118
Old Style 118
Olivetti 118
Onionskin 119
Open Type 119
Optical character recognition 119
Orphan 119
Ortelius, Abraham 119
Oxford Comma 119
Oxymoron 119

P

P22 Type Foundry 121
Palaeography 121
Palatino 121
Palmer, Volney 121
Pangram 121
Pantograph 121
Panton, Verner 121
Papanek, Victor Joseph 121
Paper 122
Papyrus 122
Parent sheet 122
Pasche, John 122
Password 122
Patria 122
Paul, Arthur 122
Paulin, Pierre 122
PDF 123
Peace Symbol, the 123
Pencil of Nature, the 123
Penny Black, the 123
Perriand, Charlotte 123
Perri, Dan 123
Peru 124
Pesce, Gaetano 124
Pfund, Roger 124
Phénakisticope, the 124
Phototypesetting 124
Pica 125

Pictogram 125
Pi font 125
Pigsty 125
Pilcrow, the (¶) 125
Pineles, Cipe 125
Pioneer plaque, the 125
Pixel 126
Plakatstil 126
Plantin 126
Plantin-Moretus Museum 126
PNG 126
Point 126
Ponti, Gio 127
Porsche, F. Alexander 127
Potaka 127
PPI 127
Preetorius, Emil 127
Primary olours 127
Printer's Devil 127
Printer's mark 127
Proforma 128
Prouvé, Jean 128
Puiforcat, Jean 128
Push Pin Studios 128

Q

Q 130
Quarter Binding 130
Quarto 130
Quasar 130
Quire 130
Quistgaard, Jens 130
QWERTY 130

R

Raacke, Peter 132
Race, Ernest 132
Radio Nurse 132
RAF 132
Rainbow Fountain 132
RAL 132
Rambow, Gunter 132

Rams, Dieter 132
Rand, Paul 134
Ray Ban 134
Ray Gun 134
Reading Speed 134
Rearview Mirror 134
Rebus 134
Red Cross 134
Red-green colour blindness 134
Reed, Ethel 135
Reichel, Hans 135
Reich, Lilly 135
Reid, Jamie 135
Reuters 135
RGB 135
Rietveld, Gerrit Thomas 136
Rimowa 136
Risom, Jens 136
River 136
Rodchenko, Alexander 136
Rohde, Gilbert 136
Rohe, Mies van der 136
Rolling Stones, the 137
Roman Type 137
Roos, Sjoerd Hendrik de 137
Rosetta Stone, the 137
Rossum, Just van 137
Rotunda 137
Roundel, the 138
Rügerin, Anna 138
Rupee 138
Russell, Gordon 138

S

Saarinen, Eero 140
Saatchi & Saatchi 140
Sabon 140
Sacco 140
Sagmeister, Stefan 140
Saladino, Gaspar 140
Sans-Serif 141
Sapper, Richard 141
Sasson, Steve 141
Savignac, Raymond 141

Saville, Peter 141
Sawyer, Tom 142
Scala 142
Scarpa, Carlo 142
Schawinsky, Alexander 142
Schelter & Giesecke 142
Schirner, Michael 142
Schlemmer, Oskar 142
Schütte-Lihotzky, Margarete 142
Screen Printing 143
Semiotics 143
Sender, Sol 143
Senftenberg Egg, the 143
Serif 143
Set solid 143
Shakers, the 143
Sharp, Martin 143
Sherbow, Benjamin 143
Shirley Cards 144
Shoulder 144
Skeleton black 144
Slab serif 144
Small Caps 144
Smiley 144
Snow White's Coffin 144
Soft Sell 145
Spam mail 145
Spanner, Russell 145
Spiegel 145
Spiekermann, Erik 145
Spine (Bookbinding) 145
Spine (Typography) 145
Spur 145
Stam, Mart 145
Starbucks 146
Starck, Philippe 146
Steinweiss, Alex 146
Stem 146
Stewardesses 146
Stölzl, Gunta 146
Stone, Sumner 146
Štorm, František 146
Straub, Marianne 146
Streamline Moderne 146
Streisand, Barbara 146
Strike, Lucky 147

Studio 65 147
Stylorouge 147
Subscript 147
Subtractive colour 147
Subvertising 148
Sullivan, Louis H. 148
Sum 148
Superellipse 148
Supergraphics 148
Supermarket principle 148
Superscript 148
Superstudio 148
Sutnar, Ladislav 148
Swash 150
Swastika, the 150
Sweden 150
Swedish alphabet 150
Swiss Punk 150
Symbol Sourcebook, the 150
Syniuga, Siegfried Michail 150
Syntax 150
Szekely, Martin 150

T

Tail 152
Talbot, William Fox 152
Tale of Genji, the 152
Tallon, Roger 152
Tattoos 152
Teague, Walter Dorwin 152
TED 152
Terminal 152
The Face 152
The Who 152
Thinking Man's Chair 153
Thompson, Bradbury 153
Thonet, Michael 153
Thorowgood, William 154
Thumb index 154
Thumbnail 154
Thun, Matteo 154
TIFF 154
Tiffany Blue 154
Time 154

Index

Times New Roman 154
Times Roman 154
Tironian notes 154
Title page 154
Tittle 154
Tofu 154
Tokyo 155
Tomato 155
Tombstone 155
Toscani, Oliveiro 155
Total Design 155
Tracking 155
Trademark 155
Trade Marks Registration Act 155
Transliteration 155
Trojan Room coffee pot 156
Trubridge, David 156
True Alphabet 156
Tschichold, Jan 156
Tufte, Edward 156
Tuvalu 157
Twen Magazine 157
Twombly, Carol 158
Type Case 157
Typeface 157
Type Foundry 157
Type size 157
Type sizes 157
Type specimen 157
Typography 157

U

Umeda, Masanori 160
Uncial script 160
Uncoated Paper 160
Unicode 160
Unigrid System 160
Unity symbol 160
Univers 161
Universale 161
Unknown Pleasures 161
Upper and lower case 161
Uppercase 161
Urquiola, Patricia 161

V

Vacat Page 163
Vaio 163
Vantablack 163
Vaporware 163
Varnish 163
Vector Graphic 163
Vega, Arturo 163
Venus 163
Ver Sacrum 164
Verso 164
Vetter, Hans Adolf 164
Victore, James 164
Victoria and Albert Museum 164
View from the Window … 164
Vignelli, Massimo 166
Visorium 166
Vocabulary 166
Vogue 166
Voormann, Klaus 166
Voyager Golden Record, the 166

W

W 168
Waldi 168
Walker 168
Wanders, Marcel 168
Warde, Beatrice 168
Washi 168
Watermark 168
Watts, Charlie 168
Weber, Kem 169
Website 169
Wedgwood, Thomas 169
Wegner, Hans Jørgensen 169
Weidemann, Kurt 169
Weight 169
Weil, Daniel 169
Well, Darius 171
Werkman, Hendrik Nicolaas 171
West, Jerry 171
Westminster 171
White space 171

Widow 171
Width 171
Wilanów Poster Museum, the 171
Wilder, Billy 171
Wilp, Charles Paul 171
Wilson, Robert 172
Windsor 172
Wittgenstein, Ludwig 172
Wittkugel, Klaus 172
Wobo 172
Wolfe, Tom 172
Wonderground Map, the 172
Woodcut 174
Word frequency 174
Word of the Year 174
World Design Capital 174
Worm 174
Wove paper 174
Wright, Frank Lloyd 174
Wright, Russel 174
WYSIWYG 174

Zwart, Piet 178
Zyzzyva 178

X

x-height 176
Xylography 176

Y

Yanagi, Sori 176
Yellow 176
Yellowing 176
Yes Men, the 176
Yo 176
Yokoo, Tadanori 176
Yoshioka, Tokujin 176

Z

Zanuso, Marco 176
Zapf, Hermann 176
Zaum 176
Zündapp Janus 178

Colophon

BIS Publishers
Building Het Sieraad
Postjesweg 1
1057 DT Amsterdam
The Netherlands
T +31 (0)20 515 02 30
bis@bispublishers.com
www.bispublishers.com

ISBN 978 90 6369 455 5

Written, edited and designed by
Ralph Burkhardt

Typeset in
Futura and New Century Schoolbook

About the Author
Ralph Burkhardt is a designer, author, lecturer and Member of aed Stuttgart, born in 1980. He studied Information/Media at the University of Design in Schwäbisch Gmünd and graduated with his diploma project called "Rotis – A polemic paper", which was published in 2006. He acquired expertise at büro uebele and Jung von Matt and became managing partner of burkhardthauke in 2009, which has been awarded with several national and international design prizes. Since 2012 he teaches typography at the Media University (HdM) and holds lectures in various countries. In 2015 he wrote an extensive design practice book for communication designers, called "Printdesign". In 2016 he founded a second company called burkhardtschwarz – Laboratory which focuses on the interface of design and art.

www.burkhardthauke.de
www.burkhardtschwarz.de